I Remember Myrtle Beach When …

A Collection of Local History, Personal Stories, Photographs and a Brief Biography of Dr. J. Marcus Smith

Edited By

J. MARCUS SMITH, JR.

August 2013

Copyright © 2013 J. Marcus Smith, Jr.

All rights reserved.

ISBN-13: 978-1482798623

DEDICATION

I dedicate my father's personal stories, photographs and his biography to the loving memory of him. Dr. J. Marcus Smith was very much a family man. He and our mother, Frances Marian Johnson Smith, raised three of us boys – me, Frank and David. He was a people person, and he knew nearly everyone in the area for so many years. He was affectionately called "Pop" by his family, particularly his six grandchildren. The fact that he knew nearly everyone was not lost on my two boys. When we were out as a family and I happened to speak to many people, my boys would bring me right back to earth saying, "You are a 'Pop Wanna be.'" That is a great role to aspire to in life.

Dad passed away on May 16, 2008 – just over three years after Mom had died. He was never quite the same after her death. As our former pastor Rev. Ken Timmerman, has said, "When you are married, two become one and when one dies, you are only a half."

Dad and Mom, we love you and miss you.

J. Marcus Smith, Jr.

August 2013

CONTENTS

Preface

Acknowledgments

I. Introduction to Horry County   1

Census of 1850 • Independent Republic of Horry

II. Early History of the Grand Strand Area   8

In the Beginning • Early Myrtle Beach • Grahamville to Singleton Swash • Withers Eight-Mile Swash • Shell Community of Horry County

III. The Early Days   1900s & 1910s   36

Arrival of the Shoo-Fly Train • Turn of the Century Train • Conway Lumber Company • Conway Hospital • Trip to the Beach • Long Tall Sand Dune • The Gathering Place • All Aboard from Homewood • Horry County Sheriffs • Christmas in Myrtle Beach

IV. Beginning of the Resort Era   1920s   61

Marcus & Frankie's Bio (20s) • Roads to Myrtle Beach • Myrtle Beach Theaters • Early Boardwalk • James Henry Rice • Hart's Esso • Ocean Forest Hotel

V. A City Emerges   1930s   79

Marcus & Frankie's Bio (30s) • Show Boat A-Coming • Tarzan's Cabin • Looking At the Past • During the Depression • Early Myrtle Beach Police Force • Fire Department • Number Please • Mayors of Myrtle Beach • Old Beach Road • Eason's Store at Murrells Inlet • Myrtle Beach's First Football Team • Yaupon Swash • Nye's Drug Stores • Post Office • Myrtle Beach Newspapers • Rourk Brothers • It's A Girl • Patricia Inn • Ocean Plaza Hotel • Archibald Rutledge • Harness Horse Racing • Let's Go Crabbing

VI. The War Years   1940s   138

Marcus & Frankie's Bio (40s) • *Conway Theaters* • *A Spy on the Beach* • *Myrtle Beach's First Airport* • *Mr. Joe White* • *Summer of 1942* • *Arcade Lunch Room* • *Guest and Boarding Houses* • *Highway 501* • *Horse Racing Returns*

VII. The Innocent Years   1950s   168

Marcus & Frankie's Bio (50s) • *Carolina Circle Theater* • *The Miss South Carolina Pageant* • *End of Summer* • *Coastal Carolina College* • *Hurricane Hazel* • *Myrtle Beach Meets Myrtle Beach* • *1957 Sun Fun Festival* • *Return of the Braves*

VIII. The Growth Years   1960s – 1990s   193

Marcus & Frankie's Bio (60s – 90s) • *Seems Like Yesterday*

IX. Today and Tomorrow   2000s and the Future   200

Marcus & Frankie's Bio (2000s) • *Final Thoughts*

PREFACE

My Dad had all intentions of publishing his collection of personal stories of Myrtle Beach before he died. He had a tough time in thinking through the articles and the book in his later years. In his many years of writing, he made the transitions from typewriter to word processor to Word Perfect to Microsoft Word. He loved his typewriter, and he never truly embraced the personal computer, but he did try. He did get his stories in electronic format, but he did not get to polish a few of them.

It has taken me a while to get to the point of compiling all his stories. Then it occurred to me during an afternoon walk that his life experiences and personal stories were more than just contents in a book – his biography (a short one anyway) was needed to be woven into the book. A book of his life and writings, along with some photographs, would provide a treasure chest of memories for many people. These brief sections of biography for Marcus and Frankie were written by me.

Now for a few moments of personal pride... Dad was a fine man and gentleman. He and Mom were always there for the three of us – be it ballgames (which were a lot over the years), PTA meetings, school activities, church functions and anything else that we happened to be involved in doing. They were great parents and role models. They always had our house open to anyone who dropped by. Hot dogs were always served on Saturday for lunch, and we never knew who might come by. Our friends were welcome to come over any time – to hang out, play baseball, play ping pong, shoot basketball or fish in the lake. Of course, you would have to endure some of Dad's practical jokes and hear his corny jokes and stories. They don't seem so corny now.

Dr. Marcus, as he was called by many, loved people and he loved his hometowns – Conway and Myrtle Beach. The history of both cities blends together in his life. Here are some stories that can take people back in time, and as Dad would say -- "I remember Myrtle Beach When..."

Dad wrote most of his stories from his own experiences in growing up in this area, and they carry the flavor of much personal interaction – identifying with many people. Most of his articles/stories were published in *The Sun-News*. The newspaper articles were usually edited significantly. So, some of the stories in the book will have more personal descriptions and details than you read in the newspaper. Many stories were written several years ago (and I haven't changed the format), so you will feel as if you are reading them as they just happened. In this collection of articles there are many places of overlap, as each article was written to stand on its own.

Dad and I had worked for quite a while on how to lay out the history and stories for this book. We had determined that a history of Myrtle Beach would not be complete without an understanding of the history of Horry County and the city of Conway. He had done a great deal of research on the history of the area, and he pulled information from many sources. I do not have the sources of all his material, so I will not be able to footnote the documentation. Some of his stories and notes were taken from talks he gave to various groups, so the presented material may flow in outline note form. Other information was obtained through conversations and interviews with many acquaintances, friends and neighbors.

We had decided to group the history and stories by decade, so that you could see the city of Myrtle Beach grow and develop. Dad had also written a number of articles on Conway, and we had discussed putting them in another book. But time was not on our side, and I have decided that the story of his life and the area would not be complete without including those Conway stories. So you will find yourself going back and forth between Conway and Myrtle Beach. We decided that we would include stories and history through the 1960s, as the nature of Myrtle Beach was changing from the small town that Mom and Dad knew and loved to a seaside resort area.

J. Marcus Smith, Jr.

ACKNOWLEDGMENTS

There are many people who were helpful to Dad in pulling together his information for stories. Dad wanted to be sure that he had the facts before publishing any articles. Listed below are a few of these many people. Dad would have struggled to put this list together, as he would have been afraid that he would have left someone out, and he would never want to do that.

Catherine Lewis – Catherine was a librarian for the Horry County Library for many years, and she was pretty much Horry County's historian. She wrote articles for *The Sun-News*, just as Dad did. She was the leader for Leadership Conway when I was a participant in the early 1980s. She loved the history and the stories of this area. She and Dad shared this love of Horry County, Conway and Myrtle Beach. Catherine gave Dad some of her information on the local history, and that meant a great deal to him.

Blanche Floyd – Blanche was another local historian of the area. In fact, she taught me in the 8th grade – South Carolina History. She also wrote articles for *The Sun-News*. She was always telling Dad to write his book. She would review his articles before he turned them in to the newspaper – and she would critique them as only a school teacher could – with love and a careful eye. Dad took her criticism well and her comments helped him to become a better writer. She and her husband, J.K., were true and dear friends of Mom and Dad. Blanche passed away in January of 2008. J.K. passed away in October of 2012.

Jack Thompson – Jack is a local professional photographer who was a close friend of Dad's for many years. Jack had told Dad many years ago that he would let Dad use any of his photographs when he wrote a book. Jack has been so gracious as to offer some of his photographs for this book. It is an honor to have Jack's photographs in Dad's book.

Dixie Dugan – Dixie is a local artist. She worked with Dad on many occasions as Dad tried to paint – but writing was his creative skill. Dad collected many of Dixie's paintings, which my brothers and I now treasure. Dixie gave permission to use one of her paintings as the jacket for this book. Thank you Dixie.

First United Methodist Church – My father was very active in our church for many years. But his passion was in teaching the youth in Sunday School and in Methodist Youth Fellowship (MYF). He prepared hard and well for the lessons he wanted to deliver to the young people. He also let them be kids. The three of us boys always looked forward to seeing the crazy teenagers coming over to the house for some party in our backyard. He was involved in the MYF from the early 50's to the late 60's. This would have been work to others, but he loved it and it kept him young. He served as an adult friend to many of the youth, who sought his wisdom and guidance. This investment of time helped him in his future research, as well as providing him with energy and with many wonderful stories.

I could not have pulled this manuscript together without the careful editing eye of my wife Sherry. She was extremely helpful in reading these stories and helping with the flow and consistency of Dad's words.

And to the many other people who have spent time with Dad – either giving him some pointers in writing, providing him with information on the history of the area, or giving him personal stories of the area and of their families. Dad loved people and he loved to talk. Thank you everyone.

J. Marcus Smith, Jr.

I. Introduction to Horry County Census of 1850

In 1995, *The Independent Republic Quarterly ("IRQ")*, published by the Horry County Historical Society, contained interesting facts on Horry County in the mid-1800s.

In 1980, Janet H. Woodward compiled information from the 1850 Census of Horry County. The late Sterk Larson had entered the facts into a database for publication in the quarterly. The data was subject to various checks to insure accuracy against the original volume. (Spelling not corrected.)

Occupations for 1,032 persons were listed: farmers (934), school masters/teach school (13), merchants (11) and day laborers (11) headed the list.

Others included: carpenters (7), coopers (7), lawyers (4), mechanics (4), blacksmiths (4), overseers (4), doctors (3), seafaring (3) and tailors (3). The register continued: accountant/book-keeper (2), engineers (2), millrights (2) and wheelwrights (2).

One each for the following occupations: turpentine distiller, ferryman, hotel operator, jailer, miller, ship carpenter, shoemaker, surveyor, turpentine gatherer and wagoner.

Regarding the birthplace of 5,568 people, 380 or 6.8 percent were born out of state. Included are: North Carolina (344), Maine (10), Mississippi (4), Connecticut (3), England (3), New York (3), Massachusetts (2), Ireland (2), Scotland (2) and Virginia (2). Alabama, New Hampshire, Pennsylvania, Holland and Germany recorded (1) birthplace each.

DR. J. MARCUS SMITH

According to the statistics, the population was almost evenly divided between the sexes: females 51 percent and males 49 percent.

The 10 most common surnames were: Johnston/Johnson (138), Hardee (134), Smith (133), Jordan (112), Todd (107), Floyd (104), Graham (95), Martin (90), Anderson (81), Fowler (77) and Skipper (77).

The most common female names spelled out in the census were: Mary (251), Sarah (215), Elizabeth (112), Martha (99), Eliza (75), Nancy (75), Margaret (70), Jane (69), Ann (53) and Susannah (50).

The census revealed other interesting female names. Among the names spelled out in the census were: Prudence (20), Molcey (16), Avey (15), Clarkey (14), Dorcas (14), Patience (13), Charity, Lucretia and Manthy (10) and Olif/Olaf (9). Other unusual names mentioned were: Ancey, Desdamonia, Dicey, Gatsey, Kitsey, and Nicey.

John (283) led the list of the most common male names. The name William (171) came in second, while James (169) was third. The following names completed the list: Thomas (111), Joseph (99), Samuel (95), Daniel (71), Henry (58), Benjamin (53) and George (48). Other interesting male names were: Bethel (13), Pinckney (13) and Eli (10). Also, Anguish, Colip, Furney, Ignoserous and Waterman shared the list with three each.

I Remember Myrtle Beach When ...

Independent Republic of Horry

The emblem on my 1942 Conway High School ring initiates many questions from new acquaintances. The design of the ring reveals a gold outline of Horry County. Within its borders is a boat on the water. The inscription states, "Republic of Horry." The question most often asked, "What does it mean?" I reply, "It represents the Independent Republic of Horry." Usually, the next question, "How did it get its name?"

Horry County was named for Colonel Peter Horry, patriot hero of the Revolutionary War, who served with General Francis Marion. The name is pronounced "O-REE," and newcomers and outsiders are quickly spotted if they do not say the name correctly. Oddly enough, Peter Horry never lived in the county named for him.

Horry County, with a land area of 1,154 square miles, is larger than the state of Rhode Island. It is the largest county in South Carolina and one of the largest counties east of the Mississippi River.

The origin of Conway, the county seat, began as the northeast anchor of a defense system for Charleston. In 1732, the English King instructed Gov. Robert Johnson to designate eleven townships of 20,000 acres each to be laid city. The township on the Waccamaw River was first named Kingston, later to become Conwayborough, and then shortened to Conway in 1883.

In 1734, a group of young men went out on the great rivers of the state at distances of about 100 miles from Charleston. Settlements were to be made to form buffer zones against Indian raids and to develop strong communities to support the port of Georgetown. They boated up the Waccamaw as far as Bear Bluff. Accounts of their trip indicated no evidence of any settlement in the territory. They returned to Kingston Bluff and camped on the banks of the Waccamaw. They killed and barbecued a bear and established what has become a deeply entrenched tradition...the first recorded Horry County barbecue.

In spite of the gradual increase in the number of settlers in the vicinity of the proposed town of Kingston, the second attempt failed in 1783 to establish a township. The American Revolution did not faze the inhabitants. General Francis Marion's men no doubt prowled the swamps along Horry's borders. Marion's guerrilla type of campaigning appealed to the few independent-minded men who joined his forces.

After the Revolution, a large land grant was made to Colonel Robert Conway, who served under General Francis Marion (The Swamp Fox) in the War. Later, he was referred to as General Conway.

After moving to his newly acquired real estate in 1787, he soon became one of the region's most influential citizens. In 1801, the General Assembly changed the name of Kingston District to Horry.

As the settlement developed, the tiny village was renamed Conwayborough in honor of Robert Conway. Many of his descendants still live in the county. Conwayborough, the county seat, became the site of a circuit court. Court first convened in March of 1803. A carnival-like atmosphere surrounded the judiciary sessions. People attended court for entertainment, local merchants held sales, and traveling shows often appeared to capitalize on the presence of the crowds.

Horry inhabitants became self-sustaining. They tapped pine trees for turpentine, tilled the soil, fished in nearby streams and married the girl on the next farm. It was a quiet life with an occasional episode of violence.

Historical articles by Dr. James A. Norton (1876-1950) are preserved in the Horry County Library. Norton philosophized about matters including the county's "primitive economics." He concluded that it was a society with little need for money. People were poor, but never went hungry. He did not have money, but he had produce to barter. He bought what he needed with a dozen eggs and paid his doctor with a ham. Per capita income in 1895 was $2.50 per year, but Horry's riches were in the land, its produce and a way of life.

Fields laboriously cleared for farming produced food crops for family use or feed and grazing for farm animals. Small crops of rice and indigo could be grown near the rivers, but few people attempted to cultivate them because of the labor involved.

The entire family had to help produce the crops: corn, potatoes, beans, peas, collards and turnips, rice, cotton and a few precious indigo plants to color homespun clothing. Stalks of sugar cane yielded syrup for "sweetenin."

All of the settlers brought their own customs, ways of life, skills and religious beliefs. Some recipes used were old country favorites: gingerbread from the Lake District of England, treacle scones from Scotland, 'tatie soup from Ireland, oxtail stew from Germany, and apple pandowdy from England. Other recipes had New World titles: Indian pudding, Boston baked beans, pumpkin pie.

But the little village on the Waccamaw River survived. People began to clear farms and settle farther inland. Subsistence farming and raising farm animals supplied their simple needs in the absence of paying jobs and trade. A rule of the settlers was: "If you can't grow it or make it, you do without." They held on to visions of better times to come.

The coastal region was swampy and marshy, with fast-flowing creeks, rivers and freshwater lakes. Many areas, called "bays," were low and boggy, unfit for cultivation or building sites, the habitat of black bears, deer and flocks of birds. Rivers and creeks teemed with fish, and jungle-like growth covered the mire. The bays got their name from the sweet bay trees or swamp magnolias found growing wild in the rich mire of these sunken bogs.

The Waccamaw River runs through Horry County, from Lake Waccamaw, N. C., to Winyah Bay at Georgetown. River traffic brought mail, supplies and travelers from Georgetown to Conway. It was the lifeline of the developing county. "Over the river" had meaning. A few ferries crossed the Waccamaw, most of them "flats" operated by families. Coastal settlement did not begin until about 1900.

The first Horry County courthouse was a frame building, never large enough or satisfactory. The second one, designed by Robert Mills, was completed in 1825 at a cost of $9,500. The bricks for the courthouse and nearby jail were made across the street on Third Avenue in Conway. It was the first brick building in Horry County and has been used constantly. It is listed on the National Register of Historic Places.

When a third and larger courthouse was built in 1908, the city of Conway bought the classic old structure to use as city hall. It has recently been restored and sits proudly on Main Street, near the foot of the river bridge.

The "Robert Mills Atlas of South Carolina," published in 1820, shows a population of 5,025 in Horry County, showing the slow growth of the isolated coastal county.

Located on the northeast corner of South Carolina, it seemed cut off from the rest of the state. The Lumber and Pee Dee rivers form its western and southern boundaries. The first narrow bridge across the Pee Dee River at Galivants Ferry was built in 1902, to replace the ferry. Gradually other bridges spanned rivers and creeks. The Intracoastal

Waterway, completed in 1936, further divided the county, but it has several bridges.

There is no accurate account of who first called this county, the "Independent Republic." Before the Civil War, Joseph Walsh, an important leader in the county, referred to James Beaty as "King of the Independent Republic." Walsh used the term as though it was common usage, not one he originated.

"Independent Republic of Horry!" The expression arose out of political disputes and because of the people's way of life, over many years of isolation.

II. Early History of the Grand Strand Area

In The Beginning

The Withers families were among the earliest settlers on Long Bay (the area between the N.C. line and Winyah Bay in Georgetown), as the Myrtle Beach area was first known. In 1765, John, Richard, William and Mary Withers each had grants of nearly 3,000 acres in the Myrtle Beach area. Withers Swash area was one of the large land grants. The Witherses were influential in Georgetown and Charleston. Perhaps, that is why they received such large grants.

At the Prince George Winyah Episcopal Church in Georgetown, a gravestone lies just outside the door that opens into the cemetery. It reads, "SACRED TO THE MEMORY OF MARY ESTHER WITHERS (Died 1801), MOTHER OF FRANCIS, RICHARD, AND ROBERT WITHERS. SHE GAVE UP THE PLEASURES OF SOCIETY AND RETIRED TO LONG BAY WHERE SHE RESIDED A GREAT PART OF HER LIFE DEVOTED TO HER CHILDREN...."

The families operated indigo plantations on their Long Bay properties. They also raised cattle and ran tar. Large forests had an abundance of fat pine lightwood (light-ard knots), which was stacked in ovens and converted to tar and pitch. The English government paid the Americans settlers a subsidy for running tar, a product much in demand for maintaining their large navy.

The Withers family built their home in the midst of a heavily wooded area overlooking Withers Swash. The house was located a short distance from the beach (near today's Kings Highway and 3rd Ave. South). During the American Revolution, the main route of travel for the

British Redcoats was through the present Myrtle Beach area by way of the strand. The undeveloped and swampy area provided safety for Mary Withers and her family.

Georgetown papers reported the tragedy of the "hurricane of 1822." Three days of heavy rains and strong winds pounded the upper Carolina coast. The eye of the hurricane passed over Pawleys Island at high tide. More than 300 people lost their lives in the violent storm.

On Long Bay (Myrtle Beach), eighteen people seeking refuge from the hurricane gathered in the Withers' home. The frame house was lifted off its foundation near Withers Swash and floated out to sea. Information handed down by word of mouth stated that the waters in Murrells Inlet were so high that dead cows were lodged in tops of massive oak trees.

It was originally known as Eight Mile Swash (the origin of the stream was probably near the present Barefoot Landing -- White Point Swash). Withers Big Swamp is the name shown for a part of modern Myrtle Beach (on U.S. government maps). A stream, known as "Eight Mile Swamp Swash," ran through Withers Big Swamp. The Intracoastal Waterway did not open until 1936. Early maps reveal that the Witherses owned almost 3,000 acres along the swamp that emptied into Withers Swash at 3rd Avenue South.

From the current location of Broadway at the Beach, the large ditches passed through this area as the swamp water headed for Withers Swash, where it met salt water. Ernest Todd told me that he has fished in those ditches and caught bream the size of his hand.

Years later, the Witherses abandoned their landholdings. The Withers name still remains in Myrtle Beach: Withers Cemetery, Withers Drive, Withers Alley and Withers Swash.

DR. J. MARCUS SMITH

The Withers' land was not purchased in one large tract. After several changes of ownership, Burroughs and Collins Company, of Conway, eventually acquired the acreage by deed dated March 9, 1881.

At one time in the late 19th century, Horry County had the largest producing turpentine industry in the country. In those years, the usual practice was to lease the land and move on. The Burroughs realized that it was better to buy the low-priced land, rather than lease. After the trees had been boxed and worked out, the operators began to move to the southern part of Georgia, the new center.

Naval stores began to disappear. A segment of the people was engaged in limited farming, which proved to be difficult. Produce had to be moved out of Horry County by water on little paddle wheels steamers that traveled the Waccamaw and Little Pee Dee rivers.

One of Burroughs and Collins' lumber camps was located in what is now downtown Myrtle Beach. Workers lived in small crude houses built away from the ocean. A small settlement already existed on the coast. Fishermen, farmers and lumbermen made up the coastal hamlet. Names of some of the families were: Todd, King, Owens, Dubois, Cooper, Stalvey, Cox, Edge, Anderson, Macklen and Collins.

The name of the post office was Withers, S.C. (1881), and Daniel J. Cox served as its Postmaster. Ernest Todd, his grandson, related a story to me. He said that everybody wanted the job as Postmaster. One morning a man needed postage money (one cent), and Mr. Cox asked him to bring the penny in later that day. The man reported Mr. Cox to the authorities, alleging that he was doing credit business at the Post Office. Mr. Cox was relieved of the duties.

Article from the *Myrtle Beach News* in 1942: J. Daniel Skipper said, "This is my first visit to this wonderful resort since 1892. Looking back fifty years, there was only one small hotel and a logging camp owned by Burroughs and Collins. I did not see any familiar faces, but I do remember Marshall Nance, a prominent fisherman." Mr. Skipper showed the newspaper editor a silver dollar dated 1876, which he received for working in the logging business. Marshall Nance, a fisherman, from the Calabash-Shallotte area, worked the upper coastal section of Horry County.

Lolly Todd and his brother, Billy, among other families, lived near Withers Swash. In addition to farming, Todd owned a fishery on the south side of Withers Swash. They worked for shares in this operation.

One day at the fishery, Mary Ellen Todd, the youngest daughter of Lolly and Amissa Mitilda Edge Todd, saw Daniel "Dan" Wayne Nance, a son of Marshall Nance. Nance lived between Shallotte and Calabash. He traveled the rugged coastal trail or by boat to court Mary Ellen Todd. A romance blossomed and they were married in 1910.

On December 16, 1965, the *Sun News* published an interview with Mary Ellen Todd Nance, then almost 72 (born about 1893), recalling her childhood in Myrtle Beach around 1900. Cedar and holly cut from the woods provided Christmas decorations, and she stated that her daddy always killed hogs before Christmas. For dinner, they had backbone and rice, biscuits, sweet potatoes and fresh fruit (fresh fruit was a luxury).

Cakes, cookies and syrup candies were a part of the Christmas menu. She said they raised sugar cane on the farm. To top it off, nearly every Christmas, she said they had snow -- in fact three or four big snowfalls annually.

The small coastal settlement was referred to as New Town. Prior to 1900, the upper and lower Grand Strand had summer visitors. New Town was isolated. To the north, Little River had a large harbor. Murrells Inlet had a small harbor to the south and Georgetown was home to the large Winyah Bay. New Town only had Singleton and Withers Swashes (Singleton Swash is at the current Dunes Golf & Beach Club).

The swashes were not large enough to accommodate big boats. Swampy land prevented much ground travel to and from the west. The steamboat, *The Comanche*, traveled the Waccamaw River from Conway to Socastee. When the boat arrived, people rushed to the docks to get mail and supplies and news from the outside world.

Socastee and Pine Island were larger than New Town. Pine Island, which was located across from the present Waccamaw Pottery stores, was a crossroads store located between Socastee and Wampee (there was no Intracoastal Waterway at the time) on a sandy rutted road. In the store, produce was sold, along with fresh eggs, etc. Pine Island had a livery stable and a large sawmill. A truck garden farm was nearby. In Socastee, Clardy's, Stalvey's and Cooper's general stores also served the needs of coastal people. Prior to 1900, people from the Conway area enjoyed a visit to Murrells Inlet and the coast. But how did they get to the coast?

A visit to Withers Swash: They traveled from Conway by horse and wagon, buggy, oxcart and horses. They traveled south on Conway's Georgetown Highway. They turned left beyond Toddville and traveled to Bucksville. Upon reaching the Waccamaw River, they continued on a river road beyond the community of Bucksport to Peach Tree Landing. Upon their arrival, they had to strike an iron pipe against a plow share that was hanging from a tree, to get the attention of the ferry operator. Once across the river, they had to cross Socastee Creek Swamp on low lying wooden bridges. In the event the water was too high, they would be unable to continue their journey. They continued on the sandy shore road to the coast and set up camp at Withers Swash.

From the *Horry Herald* in 1900, a poem under Bucksport items appeared in the weekly.

> and ere the sun had sunk to rest,
> in the shadow of the west,
> the Waccamaw we had crossed
> and left the waves on which we tossed.
> the words we heard o'er and e'er
> was again to see the shore,
> and what a pleasure it would be,
> to once more visit by the sea.

Trip to Murrells Inlet: The trip to Murrells Inlet was similar to the Withers Swash journey. According to an article by Lucille Burroughs Godfrey, she related the story about Mr. Howell and his family who spent the summer at the Inlet. The night before, they loaded their luggage on the boat at the Conway steamship terminal. The following morning, they left Conway at sunrise and finally docked at Wachesaw landing. A week earlier, they left a message for a team to meet them and escort the family to their destination. It was a tiring trip. They asked Howell if he planned to return the following summer. He replied, "It would be more convenient to send them to the Philippines."

DR. J. MARCUS SMITH

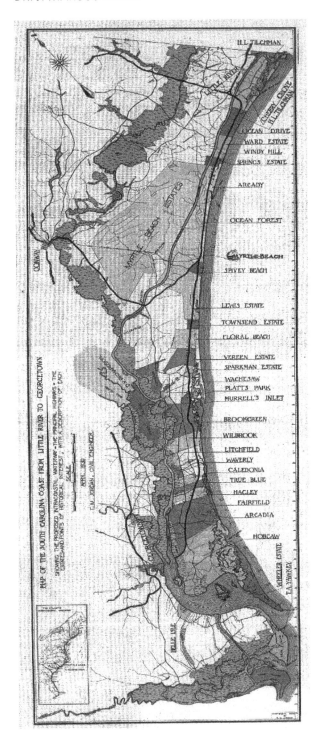

This map of the Grand Strand (Little River to Georgetown) was drawn by T. M. Jordan, Civil Engineer, in 1930.

Trip to Singleton Swash: Don and Georgia Burroughs, Lucille Burroughs Godfrey (younger sister of Don), family, friends and children made the trip. Camping supplies were loaded on the boat, *The Driver*, the night before in Conway. The boat left the docks at sunrise for Grahamville, a thriving community, located 10 miles up the meandering Waccamaw River and six miles by rugged road.

Grahamville had a store (Burroughs & Collins), turpentine still, cotton gin and a post office. Nearby was a shed where cypress shingles were made.

Summer vacationers to Singleton Swash loaded their mattresses and supplies in turpentine wagons. They traveled by buggy, horse and wagon on sandy rutted roads, which curved around bays and swamps. Riders on horse accompanied the travelers. After an enjoyable camping expedition, they returned to Grahamville, where a boat awaited them for their return to Conway.

Horry County citizens looked upon the 20th century as the golden age. For the lumbermen, virgin forests between Conway and New Town offered rich sites for timber and turpentine. However, the area had little other value, because it was almost inaccessible.

In 1896, F.G. Burroughs surveyed a straight line from Conway to the Atlantic Ocean. The purpose was to build a railroad to the coast. Burroughs died in 1897, but his three sons, Franklin A., Arthur M. and Don M., carried out their father's dream: access to new lumber interests and the beach.

In 1900, Franklin A. Burroughs, fondly known as "Mr. Frank," became the company manager. Immediately, he turned his attention to the virgin timber on the vast acreage held by the firm. Lack of transportation prevented the timber from being marketed.

Burroughs and Collins Company used the crudest tools to build the Conway and Seashore Railroad. Later, the name was changed to Conway Coast and Western. Times were hard back then. Wages were low and very little money changed hands. Construction workers tagged the rail road line: "cheese, crackers and water."

In September 1989, the *Horry Herald*, Conway's weekly newspaper reported: "The seacoast railroad is growing longer every day and shortening the distance between its terminus and the beach. It is now eight miles from Conway, leaving four miles to be completed before the summer season."

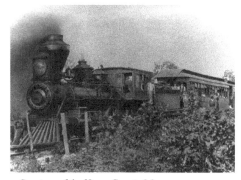
Courtesy of the Horry County Museum

The company's first locomotive was *The Black Maria*, a logging engine purchased in Tabor City, N.C. Before the first official run, the crew at New Town discovered the body of a whale on the beach in 1900. Excited Conway citizens crossed the Waccamaw River by ferry and rode to the end of the line on several flatcars. They were fitted up with cross ties, which were placed around the sides of the cars. Boards were laid across them for seats. The people walked from the train to the site of the beached whale. Eye-witnesses declared that its mouth would hold a two-mule wagon.

The train returned to Conway at dusk. Ladies used umbrellas to protect themselves from cinders from the wood burning engine. The sparks burned holes in their parasols. Through the holes, they were able to see the stars that night as *The Black Maria* went puffing home. Again, they had to cross on the ferry to get back to Conway.

Edward Burroughs stated in his memoirs that one vast sand dune started south of Withers Swash and stretched to Singleton Swash. A board road was built over the high sand dunes on 9th Avenue N. to Ocean Boulevard and north along the beach front of four or five cottages.

Burroughs and Collins became the driving force in developing New Town. A contest was held on November 1, 1900 to name the resort village. Workers from the lumber camps, villagers and guests submitted names. The winning name, submitted by Mrs. F. G. Burroughs -- Myrtle Beach -- was chosen because of the abundance of native wax myrtle bushes on the beach. The name, Edgewater, was runner-up. In 1900, a telephone line was connected from Conway to the Myrtle Beach temporary office. There was a standing joke: if you stand on top of the building and yell loud enough, you wouldn't need the telephone. The cost of the call: twenty-five cents.

The Burroughs and Collins Company cleared the streets of bushes and trees and surveyed the roads. They contracted for the building of a company store and a large tourist hotel, the Sea Side Inn.

Burroughs and Collins Company Store:

On April 18, 1901, the general store opened. It was located on 9th Avenue N., between Kings Highway and the present Oak Street. Myrtle Beach's first post office was located in the back of the store. It opened May 21, 1901 and replaced Withers Post Office.

The Seacoast Railroad tracks passed the structure. A large platform was built near the tracks, so merchandise could be unloaded directly from freight cars to the platform. The customer entrance was on the west side of the store, with a flowing artesian well nearby.

The commissary served the needs of the first summer residents in Myrtle Beach. They bought food for the table and furnishings for the family's summer homes. Before the completion of the Sea Side Inn and cottages on the waterfront, members of the Burroughs families and their friends resided in company houses.

Burroughs and Collins employed many people in their farming business. They paid them in company coins, which had to be spent at the commissary.

Sea Side Inn:

At the company Pine Island store, Jim Sanders operated the lumber company. They sawed lumber used in the construction of the Sea Side Inn and employees' houses.

The three-story hotel stood behind and between massive sand dunes in an oak grove an extended distance from the ocean. The huge sand dunes blocked all but a narrow view of the ocean. From the cupola on top of the hotel, guests were treated to a magnificent view of the ocean and surrounding forest. A lengthy wooden boardwalk extended to the ocean. A bath house was on the grounds. Like the hotel, the pavilion had a red shingle roof, grey walls and white window sills. Behind the hotel, a plank walk led to the depot and further back was the company store.

On June 1, 1901, the hotel opened its doors to the public. Mrs. F. A. Burroughs served as proprietor. C.H. Snider became the manager. The rate was $2.00 per day, which included three meals.

A report from the *Horry Herald*: (June 6, 1901)

The editor gave an account of his visit to the Sea Side Inn: Mrs. F. A. Burroughs gave us a tour of the elegant hotel. On the broad piazzas were stands of house plants giving the impression of a refined and homelike welcome. Beautiful ferns graced the spacious hallways, parlors and dining rooms.

Postcard published by Norton Drug Company.

J. E. Bryan, Sr. headed up the first Myrtle Beach development company (Burroughs and Collins). Lots were surveyed. The oceanfront was slow to develop. People still remembered the great hurricane of 1893. Stories from the past tidal wave in 1822 still lingered in their minds.

On the south side of Ninth Avenue, the first oceanfront lot was sold to A. W. Barrett, hardware dealer, of Conway for $25. In 1909, the Barretts constructed a house for $75. They named it "Idleways."

Other summer homes that followed: the home of W. A. Freeman, banker, C. J. Epps, pharmacist ("Bright Waters") and E. J. Sherwood ("the Shelter") of Conway.

Construction proved to be difficult. It was grueling hauling the timber and building materials over massive sand dunes and through heavy sand. The cottages were simply–built, offering shelter from rain and sun. Each cottage had a well or hand pump and an outhouse in the back of the cottage.

The Conway Ice Company sent blocks of ice packed in sawdust on the train to be delivered to the cottages. They used their mule and wagon. If the train arrived after dark, these men would call out "ice man, ice man" as they approached the cottages. The ladies alone with children would know who it was and not be alarmed.

About 1912, several families built a summer house north of Eighth Avenue. They were: the Hal Bucks, the James Bryans, Frank and Don Burroughs of Conway and the Richardsons of Bucksport. Later, lots were free, if you built a $500 house.

Mrs. D. V. Richardson, fondly known as "Precious," remembered that it was difficult to reach their cottage because of the deep sand. Burroughs and Collins laid a narrow plank road to their abode. She stated, "If we saw approaching car lights at night, we knew we had company. There was nowhere else to go."

In her writings, Lucille Burroughs Godfrey described conditions on the beach in the early years. Before the "no fence law," cattle roamed the beach area. A land breeze drove the animals to the water's edge to escape the intense heat and insects (flies and gnats). They waded in shallow water and waited for the wind to shift. Cows and goats nibbled on the available greenery.

"Uncle Bill Rainbow" was in charge of the Myrtle Beach sanitation department. With a mule and cart and several helpers, he made early morning rounds from the Withers Swash area with his old sow and her brood. He filled his barrels with food for his pigs. Often, pigs roamed the beach front searching for scattered food.

Simeon B. Chapin (a successful businessman):

The Chapin family lived in New York at 530 - Fifth Avenue. They had another home in Chicago and a summer retreat in Lake Geneva, Wisconsin.

The Chapin family was attracted to the southern climate. In 1912, they built a home in Pinehurst, N. C.

In 1911, Mr. Chapin visited the coastal area. He was impressed with the beauty of the strand, fresh water lakes, hunting and fishing. When Chapin was contacted about investing in land along the coast, he had the area surveyed.

In 1912, Chapin returned to Myrtle Beach and formed a partnership with Frank and Don Burroughs.

Chapin said that he could not personally help with the development of the beach, but he could supply working capital. Associates of Chapin in New York said that they could not move to Myrtle Beach, because their wives could not live in "that wilderness along the coast." Myrtle Beach Farms Company was formed in 1912.

At first, truck farming was the main interest of the Farms Company. Produce was sold to lumber camps in the area and summer visitors. The sale of lots was encouraged.

Mr. Edward Burroughs stated in his memoirs, "The Company got its name from the top of a potato barrel": As Mr. Chapin looked at the top of the barrel; he asked "what does MBF stand for? They replied that the potatoes were raised on the Burroughs and Collins farm. Chapin replied, "Let's call it the Myrtle Beach Farms Company." So, it was.

DR. J. MARCUS SMITH

In 1943, Chapin established four charitable foundations as a "thank you" to the states and communities where he had lived. In Myrtle Beach, there was the Chapin Memorial Library (1949). The neighboring Chapin memorial park serves as a beautiful location for outdoor activities.

On North Ocean Boulevard, he built a home, "Yaupon Dunes." Chapin died on January 3, 1945. Many local institutions continue to receive grants from the Chapin Foundation.

A swing bridge across the Waccamaw River in Conway was built just prior to World War I, probably about 1912. Prior to that, people had to depend on the train to reach Myrtle Beach. In the memoirs of Edward Burroughs, he stated there was no appropriation for building roads through the river swamps. Burroughs and Collins Company, Myrtle Beach Farms Company and Colonel D. A. Spivey joined together to build the bridge. Burroughs and Collins had interest in the beach area, as did Myrtle Beach Farms. The Colonel owned land (Withers Swash area) and further south.

The rugged road to Myrtle Beach, by way of Socastee, was a primitive route through swamps and bays. A growing number of cars appeared on the scene, as ox carts were getting fewer and fewer. The train still remained the primary means of travel.

In the early '20s, the Farms Company operated a big truck garden that had 500 acres in Irish potatoes, beans, beets, lettuce and other vegetables. They shipped the produce by train. Occasionally, they sold a little land. This was their sideline. Later, real estate became top priority.

With the overflow of guests at the Sea Side Inn, an annex was built near the corner of 8th Avenue and Ocean Boulevard.

In 1922, men from the Pee Dee area and Horry County built the yacht club and pier at 14th Avenue North and Ocean Boulevard. In 1937, Sam P. Gardner purchased the property and changed the name to Ocean Plaza Hotel and fishing pier. Gardner, a devout Christian and active member of the Methodist church, did not like the yacht club name.

In 1923, Myrtle Beach Farms Company, under the supervision of James Bryan, Sr., erected a large two-story wooden pavilion on the oceanfront. The pavilion joined the recently (1922) constructed boardwalk, which extended for a mile north in front of the summer cottages and a shorter distance to the south.

S.C. Press Association (three day excursion to Myrtle Beach):

On July 9, 1924, sixty press association members left Columbia (Wednesday) by train at 5:40 a. m. They ate breakfast in Florence and then traveled to Marion. The Conway group met them at the depot. Because of heavy rains, auto travel to Conway was impossible. After a tour of Marion, a special train took them to Conway via Chadbourn, N.C.

Refreshments awaited them when they finally arrived in Conway. The train then proceeded to the beach. The hotel management served a delicious seafood meal with all the trimmings to the tired travelers. The speaker for the evening, James Henry Rice, Jr. gave an address that lasted nearly an hour.

On Friday, the press group traveled to Conway by train. From there, they continued to Bucksport by auto for a watermelon cutting. Afterwards, they boarded the steamer *Brunswick* and moved down the Waccamaw River to a point near Murrells Inlet. They were treated to an oyster roast, fish fry and clam chowder. From there, they proceeded to

DR. J. MARCUS SMITH

Georgetown. The Winyah Indigo Society entertained them that evening. The following day, the members returned to Columbia by train.

Regarding James Henry Rice: His book, *The Aftermath of Glory*, was published in 1934. In his book, he stated that the most influential incident leading to the development of Myrtle Beach was the S.C. Press Association meeting in July 1924. Another of his books, *Glories of the Carolina Coast*, was published in 1925. The book is in Chapin Memorial Library.

This is a brief history to 1925. The population of Myrtle Beach at that time was 200.

Early Myrtle Beach

Most of you know the history of early Myrtle Beach...the arrival of the train, Sea Side Inn, pavilion, etc. I want to go back in time prior to 1900. A recent book, *Horry and the Waccamaw* by Franklin Burroughs, grandson of Franklin Gorham Burroughs, was published in 1992. Burroughs teaches English at Bowdoin College in Maine. Burroughs relates his six-day canoe voyage down the Waccamaw River from its source in Lake Waccamaw, N.C. to Winyah Bay in Georgetown, S.C. The Waccamaw River has a snake-like path as it passes through Horry County.

In order to understand the development of the coastal area, it is necessary to have a knowledge of the history of Conway and Horry County. Prior to the turn of the century, the river served as the main source of transportation. Burroughs and Collins established the Waccamaw Steamship lines in the early 1880s. Ships were built in the Conway shipyard. Steamship lines operated many years until the railroad took over. A Georgetown ship continued working the river until 1920.

Trips to the coast from Conway:
To Singleton Swash: In an article in the *Independent Republic Quarterly*, in which Lucille Burroughs Godfrey relates a trip to the swash: Don and Georgia Burroughs, Lucille (younger) and others made the trip. Supplies were loaded on boat the night before in Conway. *The Driver* left at sunrise for Grahamville, a thriving community located 10 miles up the meandering Waccamaw River and six miles by rugged road. The Burroughs and Collins store at Grahamville had a turpentine still, a cotton gin, a store, a post office and a shed where cypress shingles were made. Today, Grahamville is no more. It was located on a bold bluff fifty feet above the

river at the lower end of Wild Horse (today's Highway 90). In the 1950s, decades ahead of their times, people built summer homes along the river.

The summer vacationers to Singleton Swash loaded their mattresses and camping supplies in turpentine wagons. Family, friends and children traveled by buggy, horses and wagons to the coast on sandy rutted roads, which curved around bays and swamps.

To Withers Swash from Conway: Fishermen, farmers and lumbermen made up the coastal hamlet, which we know as Myrtle Beach today. Burroughs and Collins acquired most of the coastal area in 1881. Lumber camps were established in the area. Workers lived in small crude houses away from the waterfront.

Mary Ellen Todd was born in 1894, near 13th Avenue South. The Todds, along with others, made up the small settlement. Before the turn of the century, New Town was isolated. Little River had a large harbor to the north. Murrells Inlet had a small harbor to the south, and Georgetown was home to the large Winyah Bay. New Town had only Singleton and Withers Swashes, which were not large enough for boats to enter. Swampy land prevented much traveling to and from the west. Boats arrived in Socastee, which brought in supplies and mail. They relayed the news from the outside world. Socastee and Pine Island were larger than New Town. Pine Island (across from the former Waccamaw Pottery) was a crossroads store.

A sandy rutted road led from Socastee to the Wampee area. In the store, produce was sold, along with fresh eggs, etc. Pine Island had a livery stable and a large sawmill. A truck garden farm was nearby. Clardy's, Stalvey's and Cooper's stores in Socastee also served the coastal people.

Conway folks visited Withers Swash at the beach. They left Conway by horse and wagon, buggy, ox cart, horses, etc. They traveled south on Georgetown Highway (U.S. 701 South) for about five miles and turned left and arrived at Pitch's Landing on the Waccamaw River. They traveled the river road south to Peach Tree Landing. They crossed the Waccamaw on the Peach Tree ferry. Once across the river, they were five miles from Socastee. They continued their travel and arrived on the coast and camped at Withers Swash.

Conway folks visited Murrells Inlet. The trip to Murrells Inlet by land was similar to the trip to Withers Swash, but longer. Later the steamer came along for the trip to Murrells Inlet. Mr. Howell sent his family to the Inlet one summer. The boat left Conway early in the morning and finally docked at Wachesaw Landing. A message had been sent the week before asking that a team of horses meet them. To go to the Inlet in those days required a stout heart. After the summer, they asked Mr. Howell if he planned to send his family to the Inlet the following summer. He replied, "It would be more convenient to send them to the Philippines."

DR. J. MARCUS SMITH

Grahamville to Singleton Swash

In the 1880s, Horry County remained isolated from the rest of the state. River families had some knowledge of the outside world. River transportation provided a means of travel for Conway visitors, but they seldom traveled beyond the courthouse square.

For entertainment, young and old found the County fair to be the highlight of the year. In the 1890s, Waccamaw Steamship Lines staged regular excursions every summer on the river. *The Maggie* would sail upriver to Graham's landing in the morning and return under the moonlight.

Conway and other Horry County folks enjoyed a trip to the coast. They planned in advance for the outing, which could mean a journey by buggy, steamer, ferry and wagon.

Before her death in 1974, Lucille Burroughs Godfrey, youngest daughter of Franklin A. Burroughs, recorded historical facts about the Burroughs family and the coastal area and placed them in the Horry County Memorial Library.

In Godfrey's articles, she recalled the night she ate supper with her older brother Don and his wife, Georgia. They talked about the early days at New Town (now Myrtle Beach), Murrells Inlet and Singleton Swash prior to the arrival of the train in 1901 and opening of the Intracoastal waterway in 1936.

The trip to Singleton Swash was a long and tedious excursion. Most of the supplies were loaded on the boat in Conway the night before. *The Driver* left the docks at sunrise for Grahamville, a thriving community located ten miles up the meandering Waccamaw River and six miles by rugged road. It served as a center for the turpentine industry with the stills, store and boat docks.

After unloading the boat at Grahamville, the mattresses and camping supplies were placed in turpentine wagons. Family, friends and children traveled by buggy, horses and wagons to the coast on sandy rutted roads, which curved around bays and swamps. Godfrey recalled the arrival at the swash in late afternoon at low tide. She said, "We forded the creek from the present Dunes Club side. Mama rode in a buggy, and I can still hear the sand creaking as the wheels turned. The teams got in a stretch of soft sand, almost like quick sand. The men lifted us out, riding horses close to the wagons. It may not have been too dangerous, but we were terrified. It was like a western movie."

A small primitive house, 16 foot by 20 foot, with no partitions stood near the beach. Mattresses were placed on the floor and women and children stayed in the structure. Men slept in the wagons or on the sand. Myrtle bushes and scrub oaks afforded all the privacy needed.

A spring was nearby, but drinking water had to be hauled from Will Vaught's home, two or three miles north of the campsite. One driver and crew went for the water, and the others prepared the campsite. Children climbed tall sand dunes, played in the sand and collected sea shells. Adults gathered oysters and clams. The coastal waters teemed with fish, shrimp and crabs providing a bountiful supply for the campers. Food was prepared over open fires on crude platforms.

Bathing suits for the men consisted of old clothes. Ladies wore stylish suits made of thick bed ticking, high at the neck, with long sleeves and full pants gathered at the ankles. Big straw hats tied under the chin--sometimes bonnets--protected them from the sun.

DR. J. MARCUS SMITH

After a restful week at the beach, the vacationers loaded the wagons at sunrise, crossed the swash at low tide and headed home. They were delighted to find the boat waiting for them at the dock in Grahamville, a ghost town today. They were tired but happy travelers when they finally arrived in Conway, eager to tell others about their exciting vacation at the beach.

Withers Eight-Mile Swash

In Myrtle Beach, Withers Swash lies alongside 3rd Avenue South. The swash flows next to the Swamp Fox Roller Coaster. The Salt Marsh Channel passes under Kings Highway. It becomes Heron Pond, a larger lake bounded by 5th Avenue South and Charlotte Road. In the late 1700s, the bay of water was known as Eight-Mile Swash.

According to a 1979 article by C.B. Berry in the *Horry Independent Quarterly*, he stated that the earliest settlers on Long Bay, as the Myrtle Beach area was first known, were the Withers families. John, Richard, William and Mary each had grants in 1765 totaling nearly 3,000 acres.

Georgetown papers reported the tragedy of the "Hurricane of 1822." Three days of heavy rains and strong winds pounded the upper Carolina coast. The eye of the hurricane passed over Pawleys Island at high tide. More than 300 people lost their lives in the violent storm.

On Long Bay (Myrtle Beach) eighteen people seeking refuge gathered in the Withers Home. A sudden surge of water lifted the house off of its foundation and floated it into the swash and out to sea.

Although the Withers families have disappeared from the coastal area, the Withers name still remains in Myrtle Beach: Withers Cemetery, Withers Drive, Withers Alley and Withers Swash. In 1881, the Withers Post Office was established.

The Dusenbury and Sarvis Company, who operated out of Socastee, accumulated the Withers properties and conveyed them to Burroughs and Collins in 1881.

Old maps as well as the current U. S. Government Quadrangle map show Withers Swamp or "Withers Big Swamp" as the name shown for a large segment of modern Myrtle Beach. A twisted stream, known as

"Eight-Mile Swamp Swash," was so named because it was eight miles from its origin to the Atlantic Ocean. It passed through Withers Big Swamp. The source of the stream was probably near the northern borders of the Withers land.

The narrow stream emptied into many large ditches in the neighborhood of Broadway at the Beach. Ernest Todd, a native of Myrtle Beach, told me that he fished in some of those ditches and caught bream the size of his hand.

The swamp water drained from the uplands and continued its way to Withers Swash where it mixed with salt water coming in from the ocean at the foot of 3rd Avenue South. Drainage was a major problem in Withers Big Swamp and the coastal section. On the Grand Strand, five other swashes faced the Atlantic Ocean: Deephead, Cane Patch, Singleton, White Point and Midway.

In 1930 Thomas C. Dunn's dream of an inland waterway became a reality. The U.S. Corps of Engineers began to acquire rights of way through the county for an Intracoastal Waterway.

The Corps dug a waterway 90 feet wide and 8 feet deep through high ground from Little River to Socastee Swamp. This section completed the project from New England to Florida. Three drawbridges replaced the temporary fixed bridges at Socastee, Pine Island and Nixon's Crossroads. There was a ceremonial opening at Socastee Bridge on April 11, 1936.

The Waterway drains much of the area, dispersing some swamps and swashes. The lay of the land is still the same, but the coastal drainage has changed.

Shell Community of Horry County

Horry County's Shell community, nine miles northeast of Conway on Highway 905, was home to less than 100 people prior to 1900.

Six landings: Gibb's, Faulk, Board, Shell, Cain's and Sandy Beach on the west side of the nearby Waccamaw River played an important role in the growth of the settlement.

The train entered the county in 1887. Genuine towns emerged along the railroad. Communities on the river were still thriving. Board Landing became the main port on the upper Waccamaw for inland stores. Records indicate that I. Williams became Board Landing's postmaster in 1885.

Frontis Hardee, a Shell native, recently introduced me to John B. Lewis and his wife, Mackie Effel, longtime residents. We visited in their home on Highway 905 by his old home site.

In a recent copy of records from the National Archives, I read the list of Shell postmasters. The first one, Henry L. Smith was confirmed February 1, 1900. Mrs. Lewis' father once served as postmaster. The journal verified that he, Bailey M. Chestnut, took office on November 24, 1906.

Lewis confirmed and added information to the article that his brother-in-law, the late Austin Todd, wrote for the *Independent Republic Quarterly* in 1980.

In the early 1900s, the turpentine business was on the way out, and people were turning to farming. During the winter, they cut and hauled logs from the woods to the river with a mule or ox team and log carts. The logs were bound or "rafted" together and floated downstream to the mill.

Farmers bought fertilizer and supplies in Conway. From Burroughs and Collins' Waccamaw Steamship Line, *The Ruth* delivered orders to

Board and Cain's Landing. Merchandise for the neighborhood stores of B.M. Chestnut and Will Sarvis came up the Waccamaw and unloaded at the warehouses on the docks. Chestnut's store housed the post office.

Charlie Johnson dammed up Mill Branch near the Waccamaw River. He built the area's first water powered grits mill. Hominy grits and meal were ground from the corn that folks brought to his establishment. Today's Mill Branch Road sign shows the whereabouts of the former mill.

Across the highway from Bethlehem Baptist Church, trees and undergrowth cover the earlier road that led to Board Landing, where people gathered for river baptizings.

After World War I, tobacco still proved to be the main money crop. The truck garden market disintegrated. River boating disappeared and crossroad stores had to haul merchandise over unpaved roads. RFD (Rural Free Delivery) replaced the little post offices in country stores scattered around the county.

The original sandy Shell Road curves east behind the present Shell Fire Station and exits to the main highway. Lewis said, "In earlier years there was a store on that road, also the Shell Grammar School that I attended."

Hardee attended Eldorado Elementary School several miles away on Fowler Road near Highway 66, which was called the Whiteville road in earlier years. He completed his education at Conway High School. After the two grade schools were closed, students from that section were assigned to Kingston Elementary School in 1953.

Homes have been built on the dirt roads that lead to the Waccamaw River. All country roads received new names for the convenience of emergency services, available by calling 911. Road signs in the community bear the names of former landings that no longer exist as they did in the early 1900s. Only memories.

III. The Early Days (1900s & 1910s)

Arrival of the Shoo-Fly Train

Four hundred inhabitants of the unincorporated village of Conway witnessed the arrival of the first train to their area on December 15, 1887. The wood burning locomotive, *The Shoo Fly*, with clouds of black smoke and white steam, moved slowly through the borough.

The Wilmington, Chadbourn and Conway Railroad had obtained permission from the Horry County Board of Commissioners to lay its tracks 1,500 feet through the business district. The tracks entered Main Street between Fifth and Sixth Avenues and terminated beyond Second Avenue on the banks of the Waccamaw River.

On April 10, 1967, the late Brigadier General Hoyt McMillan, Marine Corps retiree, who served as postmaster of Conway from 1967 to 1974, presented a brief history of railroads to the Horry County Historical Society.

He spoke of transportation and communication as keys to the development and prosperity of an area. He said, "During all of recorded history these factors have been paramount in the growth and prosperity of states, cities and people."

McMillan continued: "Burroughs and Collins Co. built the railroad to Myrtle Beach, which officially began operations in 1900. The Conway Coast and Western Railroad opened the door to the isolated coastal area."

Early passengers were ferried across the river to ride the beach train. In 1904, Burroughs and Collins constructed a train drawbridge across the river to Conway's downtown terminal. After the completion of the bridge, they extended the railroad to Aynor.

In 1912, Atlantic Coast Line bought Wilmington, Chadbourn and Conway Railroad. By this time, the train traffic in downtown Conway had become a nuisance.

Aubrey Johnson, my wife's brother, has recalled the bitter cold night in December 1919, when he and his younger brother, Jack, and their parents, Maude and Gurley, arrived from Dunn, N.C. Johnson said, "The train backed into Conway late at night and stopped at Second Avenue (the turntable was located between Fifth and Sixth Avenues on Main Street). Mother's father, Robert O'Neil Hendrick, pastor of Cedar Grove Baptist Church, was unable to meet us until the next morning. We spent the night at the Conway Hotel."

Prior to the death of Flossie Morris, at the age of 103 in 1997, Esther H. Graham visited her at the Conway Nursing Center. Graham asked her about early trains in Conway. Morris said, "In the early 1920s, I taught school in Aynor. Commuting by train to a county teachers meeting proved to be the easiest means of transportation. When we arrived in Conway, we hastily departed from the coach. The conductor scolded us for not allowing him to properly escort us off the train."

Mrs. A. J. (Virgil) Baker moved to Conway in 1925. Baker, a friend of my parents, recently told me, "Deep sand ruts made walking difficult in downtown Conway. Trains were constantly coming and going, and they made lots of noise."

By 1926 an average of ten trains, noisy and dirty, passed over the downtown tracks daily. They began to interfere with pedestrian and automobile traffic.

In the late 1920s, W. D. (Buddy) McCormack's grandfather visited them in Conway. The aged gentlemen, with a hearing problem, escorted the grandchildren through the business district. McCormack said, "He did not hear the whistle of the approaching train, so we pulled him across the tracks."

Helen Lathan Sessions said, "As a child I remember that it often rained and mud puddles were everywhere. When we walked from Jerry Cox Co. to Platt's pharmacy, we had to cross the train tracks on a muddy Main Street. We did not have boots and my shoes were always wet."

In 1928, the town of Conway waged a legal battle with the Atlantic Coastline Railroad. A decree from the U.S. District Court required them to relocate the tracks one-quarter mile east of the business district.

Downtown Main Street became a peaceful and attractive shopping center and a market town for Horry County.

Turn of the Century Train

A new century...the 20th. Horry County citizens looked upon the 1900s as a golden age. Conway, with a population of 705, had settled on the western bank of the Waccamaw River, which isolated the coastal region from the rest of the County.

The railroad, along with the telegraph came to Conway in 1887. The telephone, invented in 1876, slowly made its way into the County.

The sleepy little village on the coast, referred to as "New Town," began in an area on Long Bay, between Little River and Georgetown. For the lumberman, virgin forests between Conway and the New Town offered rich sites for timber and turpentine. It had little value because it was almost inaccessible.

In 1896, F.G. Burroughs surveyed a straight line from Conway to the Atlantic Ocean, to build a railroad to the coast. Mr. Burroughs died in 1897, but his three sons carried out their father's dream: Access to new lumber interests and the beach.

Construction of the railroad began in June 1899. By summer of 1900, the tracks had been laid to Pine Island, about one mile west of the present Waccamaw Clay Products Plant.

Travelers between Socastee and Wampee passed through the crossroads settlement at Pine Island. People from New Town shopped in Thad Elliott's store. The big lumber mill, operated by Jim Sanders for the Burroughs and Collins Co., was located there.

Rena Mae Bellamy, of Myrtle Beach, told me that her parents, Mr. and Mrs. William Scarborough Brown, were married in Socastee in 1909. The day after the ceremony, they traveled to Pine Island and left their mule and buggy in the livery stable. They rode the train to Conway and had their wedding picture taken.

Excerpts from the Burroughs family papers, by Lucile Burroughs Godfrey (*IRQ*), relates the story of the whale that washed ashore near Herle (later changed to Hurl) Rocks in 1900. The old woman who discovered the mammal had come screaming the news. From Pine Island, the message reached Conway.

Adventurous Conway people had to cross the river by ferry. Several flat cars were filled with cross ties placed around the sides of the cars and boards were laid for seats. After reaching Pine Island, they had to walk to the beach. A few traveled by wagon, to see the whale.

To protect themselves from cinders, many ladies carried umbrellas, but they were burned full of little holes through which they could see the stars that night when the wood-burning train went puffing back to Conway. Again, they had to cross the Waccamaw by ferry to return home.

For several years, passengers and freight were ferried across the Waccamaw River to trains on the other side. Ferry traffic across the river was slow, difficult, and sometimes dangerous for lives or cargo.

In the latter part of 1900, Myrtle Beach became the official name of New Town, and the arrival of the train introduced the area to the outside world. The elegant three-story Sea Side Inn opened in 1901.

Increasing traffic on the railroad showed the need for a bridge across the Waccamaw River. About 1904, Burroughs and Collins built a train trestle bridge across the river in downtown Conway. The railroad bridge made travel to the beach easier and faster.

Conway's *Horry Herald* ran the following train schedule:
Conway & Sea Shore Railroad:

    Daily except Sunday   In effect June 3, 1901

    Northbound---No. 14
    Leave Myrtle Beach.....6:45 a.m.
    Leave Pine Island......7:00 a.m.
    Arrive Conway..........7:45 a.m.

    Train---No. 20
    Leave Myrtle Beach.....2:00 p.m.
    Leave Pine Island......2:15 p.m.
    Arrive Conway..........3:00 p.m.

    Southbound---No. 15
    Leave Conway...........8:00 a.m.
    Leave Pine Island......8:45 a.m.
    Arrive Myrtle Beach....9:00 a.m.

    Train---No. 21
    Leave Conway...........5:30 p.m.
    Leave Pine Island......6:15 p.m.
    Arrive Myrtle Beach....6:30 p.m.
    D.T. McNeill, Gen. Manager

Pine Island no longer exists as it did in 1900, but it's still the end of the line for the railway system. Among other obstacles, the open railroad drawbridge across the Intracoastal Waterway (completed in 1936) prevents the train from entering Myrtle Beach.

DR. J. MARCUS SMITH

Conway Lumber Company

In 1902, Conway Lumber Company was built on 13 acres of land at the foot of Laurel Street. D.W. Draper owned and operated the small sawmill on the banks of the Waccamaw River.

Wilson Brothers Lumber Company of Pittsburgh purchased the business in 1906. Without delay, the new owners employed H.M. Ambrose, a mill superintendent in Wilmington N.C., as their general manager and secretary-treasurer. Ambrose stayed at the Sea Side Inn in Myrtle Beach until he found adequate housing in Conway for his family. The train provided transportation to and from work.

Many inhabitants questioned why a northern corporation would locate in the small river town. An article in the April 27, 1913 of *The Conway Field* satisfied the non-believers.

The newspaper reported, "The timber resources of Horry County are unlimited. Our county has managed to preserve one of its greatest assets, the forests. Within our borders are vast bounties of yellow pine, poplar, oak and gum and maple."

George N. Magrath, Sr., a longtime resident of Conway succeeded his father as President of Peoples Federal Savings and Loan. George shared with me interesting information on the lumber company. He said, "Conway Lumber Co. had the first elevated tank in Conway. It was for their use in fighting fires. In order that Conway might extend its water mains, Ambrose entered into an agreement with the town. The town could draw pressure as long as the amount of water in the tank was sufficient. In the event of a major fire, Conway was to close the valves from the lines to the town mains." Under Ambrose's management, Conway Lumber Co.

expanded into a thriving lumber industry. From a single sawmill, it eventually grew into a large sprawling complex of buildings.

In 1914, the first of several disasters occurred at the plant. A Sunday morning pre-dawn fire ravaged the mill. From the near-by Methodist Church, the constant ringing of the bell, along with the shrilling whistle from the Quattlebaum Light and Ice Company alerted the small community. An abundance of lumber on the yard allowed the facility to operate, and lumber shipments were continued. Under Ambrose's guidance, the company rebuilt and expanded its capacity.

The mill employed more than three hundred people and processed about one hundred thousand board feet of lumber per day. It operated on a ten-hour schedule, six days a week. During the golden years of the 1920s, the mill was shipping 140 carloads of lumber a month.

Ambrose built an elegant three-story brick home on Elm Street. The family moved from their 5th Avenue house into the new residence in 1924.

Libby Ambrose Jones, the only surviving member of the five Ambrose children, recently shared with me memories of years gone-by. Jones said, "During the school year, Mother served as a gracious hostess in our Sun Porch Room every other Friday night. High school friends enjoyed dancing and light refreshments."

Other disasters at the mill included the Waccamaw Freshets, today referred to as floods. The largest one occurred in 1928, when the Waccamaw River overflowed its banks and shut down operations for several weeks. A half-million feet of dressed lumber remained under water for as long as three weeks.

Evelyn Snider told me about the 1928 freshet. She said, "It was September. I was scheduled to leave for college at UNC. Since high water prevented the train from leaving Conway, I paddled my canoe from our home down Kingston Lake and around the bend to the Conway Lumber Co. I recall circling the tall stacks of lumber."

After Ambrose's death in 1937, "The Big Mill", as it was known, folded in 1944. Ambrose, a faithful Methodist, was one of the founders and first teacher of The Men's Hut Bible Class, which was organized in 1918.

Ambrose was a dedicated servant of Conway and Horry County. The two loves of his life, apart from his family, were his church and the mill.

Conway Hospital

In 1900, Horry County inhabitants regarded a hospital as a place to die, rather than to receive treatment. McLeod's Hospital in Florence was the nearest medical center.

An *Independent Republic Quarterly* article recounts a captivating story: A young lady near Bucksport developed severe abdominal pains. After home remedies failed, a doctor was summoned. After traveling miles over sandy-rutted roads to the home, he diagnosed appendicitis. The parents reluctantly agreed for hospital care.

The patient was transported by mule and wagon to Conway and remained at the doctor's home overnight. The next morning, the doctor and his helpers flagged down the slow moving train as it moved down Main Street. The patient was placed aboard.

Upon arriving in Chadbourn, N.C., the patient was transferred to another train which arrived in Florence late that afternoon. Dr. McLeod examined the patient and realized the appendix had ruptured. The patient survived the surgery. The article stated the ordeal haunted her for many years.

By 1905, four doctors had located in Conway. They formed the Horry County Medical Association. Dr. Henry L. Scarborough joined the group in 1911. He built an office-residence at the corner of 6th Avenue and Elm Street.

Dr. Homer H. Burroughs received a charter for the Burroughs Hospital in 1913. The Burroughs and Collins old "Gully Store" on 9th Avenue and Elm Street was converted into a small hospital. The facility closed when Dr. Burroughs became disabled in 1922. In 1924, Dr. Scarborough relocated his office to downtown Main Street.

DR. J. MARCUS SMITH

Dr. J. Archie Sasser, physician and surgeon, returned to Conway in 1925. The local doctors realized the need for a modern medical facility. They secured a lease on the Scarborough building. In 1926, Dr. Hal B. Holmes joined them, and they moved to the old Burroughs building. The seeds were planted for the Conway Hospital.

Hospital advocates raised $25,000 from individuals and private organizations. Duke Endowment matched those funds. Additional gifts were received after the deadline. On June 26, 1929, H.L. Buck deeded a 250 foot by 736 foot lot on 9th Avenue to the hospital. The impressive three-story brick building opened in June 1931. It served the county for over 51 years.

The new Conway Hospital opened May 21, 1982 at 300 Singleton Ridge Road between Highways 501 and 544. It was a day to remember. Philip A. Clayton, then Comptroller of the hospital said, "Ten or twelve EMS vehicles and ambulances converged on the 9th Avenue hospital grounds. They transported critical patients to the new facility across the Waccamaw River." Clayton, now CEO of Conway Hospital, continued, "I moved the mothers and their babies in vans."

As we approach the 21st century, our county is no longer the frontier of South Carolina. Horry County, the largest in size of the 46 counties, has a land area of about 1,154 square miles. It is larger than the state of Rhode Island. Today, our hospitals and medical facilities are among the best.

Trip to the Beach

In the late 1800s, brave adventurers from Conway and western Horry County traveled rugged trails through the wilderness to reach the coast. Early pioneers used the Waccamaw River, walked, rode horses and traveled by mule and ox-cart. By use of ferries, they crossed lakes and rivers to arrive at one of their favorite campsites, Withers Swash, located near the present 3rd Avenue South in Myrtle Beach.

Prior to the turn of the century, fishermen, farmers and lumbermen made up the isolated coastal hamlet, which they referred to as New Town. Many villagers lived in an area known as the "Sandridge," located between the present 17th Avenue South and 3rd Ave. South, where waters from the blue Atlantic entered Withers Swash.

In addition to farming, early inhabitants fished the waters of Withers Swash. In September, local fishermen caught the fall run of spots and mullets. They worked for shares in this operation.

Burroughs and Collins' Conway Seashore Railroad was chartered on February 28, 1899. They planned to run the line from Conway to the Atlantic Ocean at or near Withers Swash. In 1900, the first train arrived in Myrtle Beach about two miles north of Withers Swash.

The entrance to the swash wandered up and down the beach with changes in tides and seasons. Swash waters extended south for a short distance behind towering sand dunes. Larger tidal waters flowed west. The first wide curve in the swash provided a popular swimming hole, deep enough for diving.

The late Annette E. Reesor's article in a 1974 *IRQ* edition describes a baptizing in Withers Swash in the early 1920s. She said, "The minister baptized 20 or more people who had gathered at the swash. They were singing well known hymns and lovely spirituals."

In the late 1920s, D.A. Spivey of Conway, representing Horry Land and Development Co., started buying land on the south end of Myrtle Beach. They erected a pavilion at the end of 3rd Ave. South. Conway residents began to build summer cottages on the oceanfront and north of Withers Swash.

As a pre-teen in the late 1930s, many of us visited Spivey's Beach and learned to swim in the clear salty waters of the ole' swimming hole, which we referred to as Yaupon Swash. Large oak trees and yaupon bushes bordered the southern bank. A mixture of coquina and red gumbo led to the water's edge. Tall marsh grasses lined the northern side.

The late N. C. Hughes, father of Tempe Oehler, engineered the construction of the sea walls on either side of Withers Swash entrance in the early 1940s, which kept the channel flowing in one direction. Swash waters passed beneath a wooden bridge on Ocean Boulevard and another one near the ole swimming hole. It flowed under a narrow bridge on Kings Highway into Withers Lake, which is now located behind Walgreen's at the corner of 3rd Avenue South and Kings Highway, and bounded by 5th Avenue South and Charlotte Road.

Before 1970, the swash was a clean, beautiful tidal creek and lake. The water was teeming with fish, especially flounder, shrimp and crabs.

Presently the swash waters flow through the Family Kingdom, adjacent to the Swamp Fox Roller Coaster, pass under King's Highway and enter Withers Lake. Three thousand acres of Myrtle Beach's run-off water from a twenty block area, as far west as U.S. 17, drain into the lake.

The City of Myrtle Beach recently began construction on a 9-foot wide boardwalk along the south side of Withers Swash between Ocean Boulevard and Kings Highway. Plans are being considered for the extension of the boardwalk west of Kings Highway and maybe eventual use of the city owned land for a large Withers Lake Park.

As in the beginning, Withers Swash and Lake could once again become a welcome spot to visit and observe the beauty of the coast.

DR. J. MARCUS SMITH

Long Tall Sand Dune

Edward Egerton Burroughs became President of Myrtle Beach Farms Company in 1964. He stepped down as president in 1977 and was elected Chairman of the Board the following year.

Prior to his death on March 18, 1979, Burroughs, at the request of his wife Carolyn, began writing down events from the past, which he described as "Jot Down's."

Prior to the turn of the century (1900), one vast sand dune extended from below Withers Swash to Singleton Swash at the north end of the beach. The dunes continued to build up larger and larger.

The sleepy little village on the coast referred to as "New Town" developed in the coastal section on Long Bay. The area was located between Little River and Georgetown. For the lumbermen, virgin forests between Conway and the New Town offered rich sites for timber and turpentine. It had little other value because it was almost inaccessible to other parts of the county.

In 1886, F.G. Burroughs surveyed a straight line from Conway to the Atlantic Ocean with plans to build a railroad to the coast. Burroughs died in 1897, but his three sons carried out their father's dream: Access to new lumber interests and the beach.

By the summer of 1900, the tracks had been laid to Pine Island. The crossroads settlement was located between Socastee and Wampee on a sandy rutted road two miles west of Myrtle Beach. Pine Island was larger than "New Town." In the store, food products were sold including fresh eggs. Pine Island had a livery stable and a large saw mill.

Construction of the Conway and Sea Shore Railroad began in 1899. By the summer of 1900, the tracks had been laid to Pine Island.

Travelers between Socastee and Wampee passed through the crossroads settlement. In the center of "New Town," the tall dune line stood near Kings Highway.

DR. J. MARCUS SMITH

The Gathering Place

Since the early 1900s, the Myrtle Beach Pavilion has always been the hub of activity in the center of town. Three pavilions have been located between 8th and 9th Avenues.

Transportation was slow and difficult in the early part of the century. The arrival of the train in 1900 made the coastal area more accessible. The locomotive arrived from Conway. Many of their residents were among the early vacationers.

The elegant three-story Sea Side Inn opened in May 1901. It stood tall in the midst of huge sand dunes, myrtle bushes and scrub oaks. Nestled between 8th and 9th Avenues and nearby Kings Highway, the outstanding resort hotel faced the Atlantic Ocean. A depot was on the north side of the structure. A plank walk curved to the inn and pavilion.

They were connected by a 5-foot-high pier-type wooden walkway with railings. The many windows in the original octagonal pavilion allowed the sunlight to illuminate the interior. A piano and Victrola provided the evening musical entertainment. On the walls, bracketed kerosene lamps gave a flickering light to the scene. Eventually Burroughs and Collins Co. installed electric lights for the inn and pavilion. During the summer months, an orchestra of college students played for the guests. The older people sat in rocking chairs and observed the young folks as they waltzed and fox-trotted. The more daring ones shimmied.

During the winter, the Myrtle Beach Farms Co. stored soybeans, corn, potatoes and other produce in the pavilion.

After the first pavilion had served its usefulness, Myrtle Beach Farms, under the supervision of James Bryan, Sr. erected a large two-story wooden pavilion on the oceanfront in 1923. The lower floor had many large archways, which allowed the sea breeze to circulate freely.

A concession stand and open dance area occupied a portion of the floor. Later, bowling alleys were installed. The pavilion joined the recently constructed boardwalk, which extended north and south.

Northwest aerial view of the old Pavilion and downtown

The second level housed a spacious dance floor, with a stage for performing artists. A white banister separated the dance area from the spectator's section, which was filled with rocking chairs. Windows surrounded the upper level, with benches underneath. In the early 40s, the hardwood floor served as the first public roller skating rink.

The pavilion weathered tropical storms for 21 years, but on the cold night of December 28, 1944, the pavilion burned. People in Conway could see the angry, glowing sky.

Myrtle Beach Farms immediately made plans for another pavilion. The opening date was 1949, which coincided with the opening of U.S. 501 between Myrtle Beach and Conway.

The larger reinforced concrete pavilion was built to withstand hurricanes. The doors were opened as Hurricane Hazel approached the coast in 1954 and ocean water flowed through the building. Again in 1989, the open doors saved the pavilion from Hurricane Hugo.

(Photo courtesy of Jack Thompson – All Rights Reserved)

When it opened, the concession area extended from 8th to 9th Avenues, which included modern bathhouse facilities. On the second floor was a dance hall and stage, with elevated balcony seats in the back. A wide concrete walk, with benches on either side, extended south of the auditorium to the business office on the upper level.

From the beginning, the Myrtle Beach Pavilion had been a center of activity. The most recent Pavilion was torn down in 2007. The area now awaits future development.

(Photo courtesy of Jack Thompson – All Rights Reserved)

All Aboard from Homewood

On July 3rd, Lonnie H. King celebrated his 92nd birthday at his Aynor home, off Highway 319. Friends and family gathered for the festivity.

King told me about one of the family vacations in Myrtle Beach in the late 1910s. He said, "My parents, two brothers and I, along with other relatives, made the trip to the coast. We traveled several miles on a dirt road to Homewood. Since the community did not have a depot, we placed our baggage by the side of the tracks and flagged down the crawling Chadbourn, N.C.-Myrtle Beach train." The Coast and Western Railroad was sold to Atlantic Coast Line in 1912.

Prior to the 1920s, free- range laws existed. Cattle and hogs were allowed to roam freely through the country. They would often stampede when frightened by the noise and smoke of an approaching train. Cowcatchers on the front of the engine were well named and necessary. Farmers received $6.00 for each animal killed.

King continued, "The locomotive zigzagged slowly through the swampy backwoods on its way to the coast. The train traveled at a snail's pace as it maneuvered down Conway's Main Street. The noise of the approaching train alerted the few cars and citizens, and they moved to the side of the tracks. Thick black smoke saturated the business district. After leaving Conway, they crossed the Waccamaw River on the trestle bridge." The next stop was Pine Island, a thriving crossroads community, about four miles west of Myrtle Beach.

After a drawn-out trip, the family unit arrived at the resort city's small wooden terminal on 9th Avenue, near the Burroughs and Collins' commissary store. King said, "There were no paved roads in the town.

We walked across the Kings Highway and registered at the Big Hotel" (Sea Side Inn).

King recalled the long wooden boardwalk in front of the two and a half story hotel, which led to the ocean. During their weeklong vacation, the family enjoyed sun-filled days of wading and swimming in the ocean, gathering shells, climbing the large sand dunes and playing in the sand. King said, "Near a sand dune in front of the hotel was a large carcass, probably a whale skeleton. We would jump through the large bony mouth opening."

The hotel guests looked forward to meeting the fishing boats as they came ashore each day. King said, "My father loved fish. The depot agent informed him that he could take a large barrel of mullets home on the train."

Along with family and fish, they boarded the train for Homewood. Needless to say, before the fish were salted down at home, they enjoyed a delicious meal of mullet and sweet potatoes, a good southern dish.

I Remember Myrtle Beach When ...

Horry County Sheriffs

An article in the Progress Edition of *The Sun News* in 1984 provided a list of Horry County Sheriffs. The records indicated that the first county sheriff was Robert Sessions, elected in 1800. He served until 1828. Solomon Sessions took office and completed his duties in 1842, after which Thomas Sessions served until 1884.

The following sheriffs (terms unknown) served the county: J. J. Kirton, Ben Bruton, W. H. Johnson, W. I. Graham and Daniel Lewis.

The carpetbaggers appointed John Newton for a short period. The next appointments were A.B. Skipper and Frank Sessions, who died in office.

Dick Sessions held the office from 1880-90 and relinquished his duties to W.J. Sessions (1890-1900). Ben Sessions served until 1912. J.A. Lewis, who lived on the corner of 5th Avenue and Laurel Street (present site of Conway's First United Methodist Church) became sheriff in 1912 and held office until 1928. Upon his death, his widow Lillian assisted in closing the office of the sheriff. James Suggs, M.D., a grandson who lives in Marion, recently told me that his grandmother heard someone under her front porch late one night. She walked out and fired a gun in the vicinity of the steps. She encountered no more problems.

Lillian, fondly known as "Mama Lilly," spent time with her daughter Irma Askins in Marion and another daughter Elsie Suggs (W.K. Suggs) on Laurel Street Conway in Conway. The back of their house adjoined my parents' property.

John Chestnut assumed the office in 1928. Edward Sessions became the next sheriff and served from 1932 until 1940.

DR. J. MARCUS SMITH

Jimmy Lathan of Myrtle Beach, son of the late Helen Lathan Sessions, told me that his mother said, "My father liked serving as sheriff. He was proud of the long line of Sessions men."

Don Burroughs took office in 1940 and resigned in 1942. John Dix, Horry County coroner, served as sheriff for one week. Sen. Paul Quattlebaum appointed Edward Sessions for the remained of Burroughs' term.

Ernest Sasser took office in 1942 and served for 10 years, followed by John Henry (1952-1960).

The Horry County Police Force was established in 1958. The establishment of the county police caused a split role in law enforcement in Horry County, with police handling criminal cases and the sheriff and his deputies working with functions of the circuit courts.

Tom Cannon was elected to the office in 1960 and served until 1968. M.L. "Junior" Brown accepted the position in 1968 and continued in the office until 1988. Arlon Small headed the department until Jan. 1993, at which time John T. Henry was installed as Horry County sheriff

In 2001, Phillip E. Thompson became the sheriff of Horry County.

Christmas in Myrtle Beach

In 1990, Barbara Horner, the *Sun News* Librarian, found a Christmas memory while doing research for the "25 Years Ago" insert for the local history column.

On Dec. 16, 1965, the *Sun News* published an interview with Mary Ellen Todd Nance, then almost 72, recalling her childhood Christmases in Myrtle Beach around 1900.

Christmas in rural Myrtle Beach around the turn of the century lacked much of the glitter and bustle associated with modern preparations for the holiday.

According to the article, Mrs. Dan W. Nance of Seventh Avenue N. remembers that the school children had a week's vacation and decorated a Christmas tree at the school, which was located one mile from the farmhouse.

"Sometimes we would have a tree at the house," the great-grandmother remarked. She said, "Usually the only decorations we had were some holly and cedar cut from the woods. There weren't too many places to buy ornaments."

Burroughs and Collins Commissary Store in the small village of Myrtle Beach and two Socastee general stores, Stalvey's and Clardy's, were the only places to go shopping.

Lots of company always gathered around the Todd farm, which was on today's 13th Avenue South, near Beaver Road. This Christmas (1965) will be a Nance family reunion for 50 or more relatives.

"Daddy always killed hogs right before Christmas. Our menu consisted of backbone and rice, sweet potatoes, homemade biscuits, and fresh fruit. We often had these type meals on Sundays during the winter months," she mused.

Fresh fruit was a luxury back about 1900. The only time it could be purchased was around the holiday season. Mrs. Nance remembers her father buying a wooden barrel of apples, a case of oranges and sometimes bananas.

Cakes, cookies and syrup candies were a part of the Christmas meal. She said, "We raised some sugar cane on the farm and each winter we made about 100 gallons of candy, which we pulled until it was almost white. Then, we cut it into small sticks."

Nance continued, "Nearly every Christmas, we had snow. We had about three or four big snowfalls every winter."

One of the daughters, Esther Nance Gray, recalls going to Shallotte Point, near Holden Beach, to visit her grandfather Nance and other relatives who lived by the Shallotte River. In 1920, they made the trip by wagon during the Thanksgiving season and stayed through Christmas.

Mary Ellen Todd Nance died Dec. 15, 1967. All these memories will live on in the stories passed down to the dozens of her grandchildren and great-grandchildren populating the Grand Strand. Marjorie Nance Benton of Myrtle Beach said, "We are just a close-knit family."

IV. Beginning of the Resort Era (1920s)

Marcus and Frankie Smith (1920s)

John Marcus Smith was born in Florence, SC on December 27, 1925. He was actually named Marcus Redding Smith, Jr. at birth by his parents -- Marcus Redding (M.R.) Smith and Geneva Neal Ross Smith. His name was changed while he was in high school – Dad always said that it was because his mother decided that she didn't like the name. He had one sister, Hannah Ross Smith, born on June 8, 1914 in Ansonville, NC. She married John Waldon Darden, Jr.

The Smith family goes back many generations in Marion and Horry Counties. Dad's father (usually called M.R.) was one of four children born to Marcus Lafayette Smith and Sarah Hannah Smith. M.R. was born in Fork, S.C. Marcus and Sarah were third cousins, as they were both great-great-grandchildren of John Smith (c. 1710-1802).

Geneva Neal Ross Smith was the daughter of John Franklin Ross and Martha (Pattie) Kate Allen from Ansonville, NC. I have been able to trace the Ross family name back to Williamson Ross (mid 1700s), whose family came over from Scotland.

My mother, Frances Marian Johnson Smith, was born in Conway on February 9, 1926. Her parents were Franklin Gurley Johnson and Maude Olivia Hendrick Johnson. Johnson and Hendrick are good Horry County names. Mom grew up on Ninth Avenue, directly across from the elementary school. Mom had two brothers: Aubrey Lee Johnson and Jesse Willard (Jack) Johnson, who are both deceased. She also had a sister, Mary Elizabeth Johnson, who married Charles E. Bowie. Our aunt, who is called "Bebe," still lives in Myrtle Beach. Mom's back yard and Dad's back yard touched and their lives were always intertwined. Dad told the story that his family was not as well off as the Johnsons and that there was coal on Mom's family's back yard. He said that he would aggravate Mom and get her to throw coal at him, so that he could gather up the pieces and take them in to heat the house.

Geneva and M.R. Smith

Dad and his older sister (Hannah)

Mom at age 3

Gurley and Maude Johnson

Roads to Myrtle Beach

In June 1922, The South Carolina Press Association held its annual meeting at the Sea Side Inn in Myrtle Beach. Road conditions made the trip almost impossible.

James Henry Rice, Jr. addressed the convention for an hour and described the natural beauty and limitless possibilities of the coast.

Good roads to Horry County and Myrtle Beach were always put on the bottom of the list. The U.S. Automobile Association started a major outbreak of highway fever by mapping out the Stonewall Highway, a route from Chicago to Myrtle Beach, via Knoxville. The route would bring people from the interior of the country to the coast.

At that time, we did not have paved roads. The Conway-Myrtle Beach road passed through Socastee. The beaches did not have enough satisfactory accommodations.

When they distributed the travel folder showing the Knoxville-Myrtle Beach route in the fall of 1922, there was a sudden soar in the future of the beaches. Suddenly the interest of outsiders made the strand an attainable goal.

From *The Horry Herald* of Sept. 7, 1922: Conway, South Carolina, situated on Stonewall Highway, 20 miles from Myrtle Beach.

"Ample number of hotels, cafes, garages and filling stations to meet the needs of automobile tourists. Banks and modern retail stores supply commercial and shopping needs of travelers."

"Located on Waccamaw River and within 10 miles of Pee Dee River, two of the finest game streams in the South. Black bass, blue breast, perch and trout teem in deep clear streams, also duck, deer and partridge shooting in season."

DR. J. MARCUS SMITH

"Myrtle Beach, Cherry Grove Beach, Little River and Murrells Inlet are all within an hour's drive of Conway. The town is the county seat of Horry County, which has 50 miles of frontage on the beach."

"Conway has a delightful summer and winter climate. The county is rich in timber and with excellent water transportation."

The following poem, unsigned except for the initial "S" is from *The Horry Herald*, August 24, 1922. It best described the village at that time:

> This is Myrtle Beach,
> Tucked in the arm of the ocean,
> Just like a child asleep,
> Safely and securely sheltered,
> From the storms that sweep the deep.
>
> Long Bay is the name that's printed
> On maps and mariner' charts
> For this broad expanse of blue waters,
> So dear to Horry's heart.
>
> Myrtle Beach is the name as we know it.
> The name that gives us a thrill,
> Because we meet the folks from, "back yonder"
> And for each an all is good will.
>
> 'Tis just a village of a score of houses or more,
> With a hotel, a yacht club,
> And the Blue Moon tea room
> That keeps an open door.

I Remember Myrtle Beach When ...

The stand where the Sasser Brothers
Dispense iced drinks, chewing gum and sweets,
To say nothing of the pavilion,
And its revelry of jazzy feet.

So, friend, if you are tired and listless,
Or just want a change from home,
Pack your kit bag and come over,
You can find us by the wail of the saxophone.

DR. J. MARCUS SMITH

Myrtle Beach Theaters

From North Myrtle Beach to Murrells Inlet, the Grand Strand accommodates over forty movie screens. The downtown type cinemas phased out when the multi-screen theaters appeared in the area.

Myrtle Beach's first movie house emerged in the early 1920s. A few feet from the corner of 9th Avenue and the wooden boardwalk, the entrance led to a rectangular room---about 18 feet by 40 feet. The late T. Glennie Bellamy, escorted by his older brother, recalled attending a performance in the wooden building. They both remember wandering down a long hall to the room. Silent movies, with captions underneath, were projected on the small screen.

An article in the *Myrtle Beach News* (April 9, 1936) stated: "B. B. Benfield has revolutionized the major form of entertainment. Ben's Broadway, located at 811 Broadway (now Main Street), is open. The construction of the Gloria Theater on Ninth Avenue, near the pavilion, should be completed next year."

On June 6, 1937, *Parnell,* starring Clark Gable and Myrna Loy, played at the Gloria Theater. Ben's Broadway offered *Fifty Roads to Town*, with Don Ameche and Ann Southern. On Sundays, patrons flocked to the Myrtle Beach theaters. Strict S. C. blue laws banned movies in inland towns on Sunday.

Chester Todd, an employee of the theaters, recruited his brother Ernest to serve as a courier for Benfield's two theaters. He said, "When a big movie hit town, it played at both movie houses. The movie first played at the Gloria, the larger theater. After reel one was completed, Ernest would rush it to the Broadway, then reel two to the Broadway, and reel one back to the Gloria for the second performance."

I Remember Myrtle Beach When ...

Louise Springs Crews vividly remembered that as a teenager, she attended the Gloria Theater in 1937. Several days before, she had a tonsillectomy. She said "I laughed so hard during the movie that my throat started to hemorrhage. I ran to my father's office at The H. B. Springs Co., and he took me to the nearby office of Dr. Bill Rourk."

Ben's Broadway, which contained 549 seats, closed in the mid-1950s, but the Gloria Theater continued to serve the resort town until the early 1970's.

Photo courtesy of Jack Thompson - All Rights Reserved

The Rivoli Theater, 908 Chester Street, opened in 1958. The Watt Parker family built and owned the theater. The large movie house had a seating capacity for more than 1,000 people. Remember Saturday mornings at the Rivoli? For six bottle caps, you could get into the downtown theater for two hours of Hollywood magic.

Myrtle Beach celebrated the 1966 Sun Fun Festival, which had a stagecoach theme, with the Eastern premiere of the movie *Stagecoach* at the Rivoli Theater. Slim Pickens and Hollywood producer Martin Racken rolled down Grand Strand streets in the 1860 Concord stagecoach used in the movie.

The world premiere of *Don't Make Waves,* starring Sharon Tate and David Draper, took place in the theater in 1968.

Myrtle Beach had two drive-in theaters: Myrtle Beach Drive-In on Kings Highway at 13th Avenue South and The Flamingo Theater, between 77th and 79th Avenue North Kings Highway, at the site of the present Northwood Shopping Center.

In the early 1970s, the Cinema Rocking Chair Theater opened at the former location of Ben's Broadway. The Camelot Theater made its appearance at 1901 N. Kings Highway.

The days of the single screen theaters -- the Broadway, Gloria, Cinema Rocking Chair, Rivoli and Camelot -- are gone. Multi-Screen theaters arrived on the Grand Strand in the 1980s.

Early Boardwalk

In the early 1920s, a wooden boardwalk on the beachfront was a welcome addition for the 200 residents and growing number of summer tourists. In 1923, Myrtle Beach Farms Co. built a two-story wooden pavilion on the oceanfront, which joined the recently completed boardwalk. Summer cottages developed rapidly along the narrow, clay-sand Boulevard.

The boardwalk, two feet above the sand, was eight feet wide and constructed of cypress wood with sturdy guardrails. In 1925, it extended one mile north of the pavilion, but only seven lots to the south. Later, it reached to 3rd Avenue South.

A small colorful carousel, the only ride in the pavilion area, stood at the foot of 9th Avenue North and the boardwalk.

During the term of Mayor Ben Graham, the wooden boardwalk between the pavilion and the Ocean Plaza Hotel (now the Yachtsman) was demolished. The Works Progress Administration worked with the city in the construction of a 12-foot wide concrete walk. Plans were made to extend the walkway the entire length of the seven-mile beachfront.

World War II halted the project. The remaining boardwalk was maintained, but it slowly deteriorated.

Hurricane Hazel slammed into the coast early on October 15, 1954. When daylight arrived, I surveyed the oceanfront and my attention focused on the leveled sand dunes, the erosion of the strand and the absence of the boardwalk.

A landmark had disappeared, but not the wonderful memories of a walk on the boardwalk.

DR. J. MARCUS SMITH

James Henry Rice

In 1903, James Henry Rice came to Conway as the new editor of *The Field*, the county newspaper. Later on he worked with the Georgetown paper, *The Carolina Field*. As a result he fell in love with the South Carolina coastal region.

Rice was born in Abbeville County in 1868 and grew up there. After attending S.C. College (USC), he taught school several years before embarking on a journalism career at age 27. In his later years, he lived at Brick House Plantation on the Cheeha River in Wiggins, S.C.

By 1895, Rice was in Columbia, where he worked as editor of the first *Columbia Evening News*. Later, Ambrose and N. G. Gonzales, owners of *The State* Newspaper, hired him to write their editorials.

Rice visited Conway in the fall of 1898. He said, "Uncle Jerry (Honorable Jeremiah) Smith and his wife operated a hotel. Meals were $.25/day, or $8.00 per month. They gave bountiful fare, well cooked. Dr. Evan Norton had the only drug store in the county. Spivey's bank, the Methodist Church and the old Courthouse (now City Hall) were among the few brick buildings."

Much of this information came from a letter in the *Independent Republic Quarterly* (1977), a letter from Rice to Mrs. Sarah Cooper dated July 27, 1933, two years before his death.

In 1924, the S. C. Press Association held its annual meeting in Myrtle Beach at the elegant Sea Side Inn. Sixty members left Columbia by train at 5:40 a.m. for their three-day excursion to the coast. The members had breakfast in Florence and then journeyed to Marion. The Conway committee was unable to transport them to their town. Heavy rains, swollen rivers and roads made auto traffic impossible.

There was no direct railroad connection between Marion and Conway. A special train took them to Conway by Chadbourn, N.C. Upon their arrival, refreshments were awaiting the tired travelers. They finally arrived in Myrtle Beach at 6 p.m. The staff of the hotel served a delicious meal to the hungry crowd. Hoyt McMillan, President of the Conway Chamber of Commerce, welcomed the assembly.

James Henry Rice, Jr. addressed the convention for an hour and described the natural beauty and limitless possibilities of the coast.

On Friday, the press members returned to Conway by train. They traveled to Bucksport for a watermelon cutting. Afterwards, they boarded the steamer *Brunswick* and traveled down the Waccamaw River to a location opposite Murrells Inlet. After they were treated to a fish fry and oyster roast, they boarded the steamer for Georgetown. The people of the Winyah Indigo Society entertained them that evening. On Saturday, the group returned to Columbia by train.

Following the meeting in Myrtle Beach, Rice published two books. The first one, *Glories of the Carolina Coast*, came out in 1925, with a second edition in 1936. *The Aftermath of Glory* was published in 1934. Through the years Rice lectured extensively and spoke about the potential for recreational development of our strand. He also worked with wildlife conservation and served as S.C. Game Warden.

In Rice's writings, he states: "We cannot have a developed state until we reckon the coast among our assets. The coast is a healthy region. There is a freshness in the air. One gets more oxygen at sea level than anywhere on the globe."

"No man can daily watch the ebb and flow of the tide, the movement of the sea, the procession and sequence of events without being impressed with the awe of the immensities. There is visible evidence of a power beyond and above man."

Referring to Myrtle Beach in 1900, Rice said, "To know the coast is to love it...love it even in its vast silent spaces."

Time marches on.

Hart's Esso Station

In January of 2002, the weather-worn and storm-damaged building at the intersection of King's Highway, 8th Avenue North and Main Street, (formerly known as Broadway), in Myrtle Beach was demolished.

For a period of time in the late 1990s, the last occupant at that location was the Hummingbird, a one-hour photo express.

In the 1920s, Howard Ambrose sold the small triangular parcel of land to William Spivey Hart, better known as Bill Hart to coastal residents. On this prominent spot in the center of town, Hart built a filling station and named it Hart's Esso Station.

Belle Hart, a sister of Col. D. A. Spivey of Conway and mother of Bill Hart, often manned the station in Bill's absence. She was aware of the almost-completed Chapin Company near the station. From her chair in the front window, she observed the few cars entering Myrtle Beach from the west on Highway 15, known as the Conway-Myrtle Beach Road. Also, she witnessed trucks loaded with building supplies traveling north on the one-lane Kings Highway (U.S. 17) to the construction site of the Ocean Forest Hotel. Cars slowly turned at the station to travel the dirt road south to Murrells Inlet.

Patty Hart Capps, the only child of Bill and Roma Hart, and her husband J. Harold Capps were most helpful in providing information on the station.

The original gas station was partially ravaged and remodeled about 1950. The late Jimmy Tyson bought the property in 1973. Hart's Esso (Exxon) ceased to be a filling station in 1975, after serving the beach area for almost fifty years.

DR. J. MARCUS SMITH

The City of Myrtle Beach now owns the cleared triangular area in the heart of Myrtle Beach. Hart's Esso is a memory, but it serves as a reminder of days gone-by.

Ocean Forest Hotel

The Ocean Forest Hotel
(Photo courtesy of Jack Thompson – All Rights Reserved)

After forty-four years, the walls of the Ocean Forest Hotel came tumbling down. The elegant 220-room hotel, which stood 29 feet above sea level, would no longer stand guard over the beautiful blue Atlantic Ocean.

News of the planned demolition of the hotel aroused immeasurable feelings of disbelief in the community. The castle-like structure, which people referred to as the "Million Dollar Hotel," played an important role in the life of locals and visitors.

On Friday the 13th, September 1974, the 10-story center tower, flanked by two five-story sections with balconies and terraces was gone, but not forgotten.

DR. J. MARCUS SMITH

In the mid-1920s, John T. Woodside and his brothers, of Greenville, purchased 66,000 acres of land from Myrtle Beach Farms Company. They envisioned a plush resort with a majestic hotel, golf courses, freshwater lakes, residential homes, scenic forested areas on the oceanfront and hiking paths and riding trails for the horses, which would rival the playgrounds of the rich in the north. They labeled their undertaking "Arcadia." Their retreat equated with a region in ancient Greece, where peace and serenity could be found in undisturbed earthy surroundings. The dreams of the Woodsides and countless others collapsed with the stock market crash in 1929. The completed part of the Arcadian dream, the hotel and country club across the Kings Highway, changed hands and continued to operate. The remaining acreage reverted to The Myrtle Beach Farms Company.

According to the *Myrtle Leaf*, edited monthly by H.T. Willcox, the March 1930 edition stated: "The Ocean Forest Hotel opened for business on January 15, 1930 under the direction of Edward H. Crandall, well known New York businessman."

On February 21, 1930, the million-dollar fireproof hotel, with its imported chandeliers and Italian marble, celebrated the grand opening with a dazzling dinner dance...by invitation only.

Invited guests arrived from New York City -- the A.A. Ainsworths, Mr. and Mrs. J.D. Woodside, S.B. Chapin and daughter Miss Virginia Chapin, Mr. and Mrs. W.H. Parkinson and Miss Marjorie King. Other invited guests came from Georgia, North and South Carolina for the gala event.

Horry County was well represented. Guests from Galivants Ferry included George J. Holliday, Miss Emma Holliday, Miss Virginia King and Helen Hicks.

Invited guests from Conway included: Col. and Mrs. D.A. Spivey, Dr. and Mrs. J.L. Edgerton, Collins A. Spivey, Harriet Edwards and Christine Dusenbury. Others were: Mr. and Mrs. E.E. Burroughs, Mr. and Mrs. F.A. Burroughs, the J.C. Burroughs, Mr. and Mrs. W.A. Freeman, Mr. and Mrs. W.A. Collins and Mrs. H. W. Ambrose.

Representing Myrtle Beach were Col. and Mrs. Holmes B. Springs, H.T. Willcox, Mrs. W.L. Harrelson, T.A. Crook, Jr., James E. Bryan, Jr. and Ralph Reynolds. Others included: The Mark Stackhouses, the C.G. Browns, the H.H. Trices, the R.T. Costons, the F.L. Ackersons, the T.M. Jordans, the E.M. Lawtons, the L.R. Jacksons and the T.T. Stewarts.

The Ocean Forest Hotel suffered during the Great Depression, but the exquisite accommodations never dwindled. Chandeliered ballrooms, fresh and salt-water baths, extravagant dining and uniformed doormen always remained the norm.

The Ocean Forest Hotel opened for the 1940 summer season on May 28. The rates: Single room and bath, one person $5.00-$9.00, including three meals. Registered guests were extended golf privileges at The Ocean Forest Country Club, which later became The Pine Lakes International Country Club.

On the southeastern corner of the hotel, The Marine Patio faced the ocean. Guests and visitors danced under the stars on the open-air patio. An elevated covered bandstand housed the orchestras. Sea breezes drifted through the sea oats on the large sand dunes across the boulevard. In the mid-40s to mid-50s, countless visitors danced to the music of Guy Lombardo, Glenn Gray, Count Basie, Woody Herman, Russ Morgan and others.

In the 1940s, local Easter sunrise services were held on the sloping lawn on the front side of the hotel. The Myrtle Beach Rotary Club met in the south wing terrace dining room. Myrtle Beach's first radio station, WMRA-AM, hit the airways in 1948 with the transmitter and studio located on 28th Avenue North and Oak Street. A satellite studio was in the arcade of the Ocean Forest Hotel, along with art galleries, gift shops and the Brookgreen Room.

In the 1950s, the ballroom served as a stage for the Circle Theater, which brought Broadway plays to Myrtle Beach. Many local and state conventions used the hotel. As the hotel began to show its age, repair costs mounted and a shutdown occurred in 1974. The owners made a decision. The hotel had to go. Like so many other citizens, we stayed away on that fateful day. On that warm September morning, Friday the 13th, the walls, but not the memories, came tumbling down.

The Ocean Forest Hotel
(Photo courtesy of Jack Thompson – All Rights Reserved)

V. A City Emerges (1930s)

Marcus and Frankie Smith (1930s)

Mom and Dad enjoyed the simple life of Conway. He grew up at 903 Main Street – just a block away from the elementary school, which was on Main Street and across Ninth Avenue. The neighborhood kids had some great times – they loved to shoot marbles, ride bicycles, skate and put on plays – in many ways like the Our Gang/Little Rascals shows. Dad was always proud that he walked across the new Main Street Bridge with the Boy Scouts, when the new bridge was opened to the public in April of 1938 (he is the scout on the far right in this photo).

The Ross family built a summer cottage on the oceanfront in Myrtle Beach in 1925 and called it the "Ross Haven." They spent many wonderful summers at the cottage.

Dad's family lost everything in the Smith Wholesale Company during the Depression. Dad's father "M.R." was always willing to give others credit when they were in bad times; unfortunately this became part of his downfall. He then struggled with a small seed store (S.C. Plant & Seed Company). Dad's mother worked for the Works Progress Administration (WPA).

DR. J. MARCUS SMITH

Mom's father Gurley operated a grocery store in Conway for several years. He later went to work for Craig Wall at Canal Wood.

"Bebe" and Mom

I Remember Myrtle Beach When ...

Show Boat A-Coming

A headline in the Nov. 19, 1936 edition of Conway's *Horry Herald* stated: SHOW BOAT COMING HERE.

The article said, "Captain Charlie Hunter, owner of the show boat and manager of the theatrical company, which lives and performs aboard her, visited the newspaper office yesterday. He plans to bring his vessel, a well-known sight in the Tidewater towns of Virginia to South Carolina." He stated, "With two diesel tugboats, we are able to travel up and down the recently completed Intra-coastal Waterway."

Hunter added, "In the 1800s, riverboats drifted from town to town with the current. When they approached a desired landing, the troupe managed large sweeps and made fast to the shore. They fired a cannon announcing the showboat's arrival. At night, flaming torches lit the way for the approaching crowd."

A picture of the original floating theater appeared in the paper. The caption underneath read "the only showboat in active operation in the world." The article continued, "Roy Steadman's famous radio orchestra, The Kentucky Colonels, and thirty people presenting drama and musical comedy make up the company, who also act as crew. Choice front and center seats are forty-cents, while others are general admission."

In 1919, Burroughs and Collins discontinued operations of their Waccamaw Line of Steamers. Steamboats operated less frequently on the river.

Town-folks became excited when the 128-foot long boat, with a 34-foot beam, moved up the Waccamaw River and arrived in Conway for a week's engagement. The floating theater docked near the Burroughs and

Collins warehouse, among cypress and moss-laden oak trees, at the foot of Main Street.

While a jubilant crowd observed the vessel, the crew passed out bulletins. They listed the first production "The Big Shot" for Monday Nov. 23, with different programs every night.

The late Evelyn Snider once shared with me the showboat days in Conway. Snider was a faculty member of Campbell Junior College in North Carolina. Snider said, "When I arrived home for Thanksgiving holidays, I was elated to learn the showboat had arrived on our beautiful Waccamaw River. My parents and I attended Edna Ferber's musical production of 'Show Boat.'"

When my parents agreed to attend the floating theater, I could not wait for the big night. I don't recall the play, but I do remember when the performance ended, they had a special show for an additional fee. We stayed. After a few minutes into the program, they got up, took me by the hand. We made a hurried exit. Apparently, the special show revealed no similarity to a Shirley Temple movie.

Once again, Conway's riverfront has become the center of activity. Moss-laden oak trees still stand guard of the Waccamaw River. The downtown revitalization program has moved forward. Who knows, maybe a showboat boat will arrive again, but not with 40-cent reserved seats.

Tarzan's Cabin

Edgar Rice Burroughs (1875-1950), creator of Tarzan, published his first Tarzan book, *Tarzan the Ape Man* in 1912. William James Langston, a lover of the outdoors, apparently studied the works of Burroughs' numerous books and observed Tarzan's fantastic jungle-adventure movies at Conway's Pastime Theater in the 1920s.

Langston, born in 1916, grew up in the two-story white house at 219 Kingston Street. The residence faced the mouth of Kingston Lake where it joined the Waccamaw River. A rowboat was always available for his use. His father, a teacher-missionary, died in 1927 leaving his widow Marjorie Quattlebaum Langston, a 4th grade teacher, to raise the four children ... three boys and a girl.

During his high school days, William Langston and his close friend, Gene Stalvey, built a cabin in a jungle- like region on the banks of Kingston Lake. They floated lumber and materials for the cabin up the lake or hauled them overland on a logging trail on the other side of the railroad tracks. His Uncle Perry at the Quattlebaum Light and Ice Company, diagonally across the street from their residence, supplied them with nails, screws and other items for their project.

The completed hut was about 6 feet by 9 feet with a fireplace and chimney nearby. They nailed a sign over the entrance: "Tarzan's Cabin." Nearby, heavy ropes were tied on massive tree limbs. Swinging from tree to tree and over portions of the lake, Langston would forewarn all within hearing distance with the thunderous roar of the famous Tarzan yell.

Among his classmates and the local community, he was nicknamed "Tarzan." Langston, with an athletic build, stood six feet tall. His piercing brown eyes and tan complexion complimented his golden brown hair, worn a little longer than average. Langston looked like Edgar Rice Burroughs' Tarzan.

Janet Langston Jones, of Conway, the only surviving member of the family, recently shared stories about her brother William. Jones said, "He was definitely a non-conformist, and he asserted his individuality. On the coldest day of winter, he would attend school in short pants. Another day, with his arm in a sling, he was asked by classmates, what happened? His reply, 'To make fools ask questions.'"

Langston, a good student, enjoyed his high school days and the special time spent at Tarzan's Cabin on the banks of Kingston Lake. College beckoned. As a member of the R.O.T.C, he graduated from Presbyterian College.

Wedding bells chimed for William Langston and "Buff" Tanner in 1939. With the outbreak of World War II, Langston entered the army in 1941.

Jones said, "In early December of 1943, a telegram from Italy arrived from 1st Lt. William J. Jones. The message: 'I'll be home for Christmas.'" Presents under the decorated tree set the stage for the season. William did not arrive on Christmas day. While other packages were opened, his gifts remained under the tree. At the end of December, another telegram arrived: "Killed in action December 9, 1943."

Conway folks still remember Tarzan's cabin. Even though the cabin no longer exists, people, young and old still wander to the original site. They travel through the woods or up the lake by boat to reflect on days gone by. William "Tarzan" Langston was not King of the Jungle, but Conway's King of Kingston Lake.

Looking At the Past

Catherine Lewis, local historian, has compiled a Gazetteer of Horry County. Much work has gone into the project entitled, "FROM ADRIAN TO ZOAN." Lewis said, "This is a work in progress."

Maps played an important part in her research, along with information obtained from the collection in the Horry County Memorial Library, which she faithfully served for 28 years before retiring.

Maps open doors to the past. The late T.M. (Max) Jordan, civil engineer/surveyor, one of Myrtle Beach's early pioneers, drafted one which hangs in my study. The 1930 survey details the S.C. coast from Little River to Georgetown.

An insert in the document traces the Intracoastal Waterway (Massachusetts to Florida) through Horry County, which was the last portion to be completed. Geraldine Bryan Burroughs, of Conway, cut the ribbon during the dedication ceremony at the Socastee Bridge in April 1936.

Jordan's map charts the direction of the Waccamaw River as it enters S.C. from its source, Lake Waccamaw in N.C. The tributary flowing in a southwesterly direction snakes its way through Horry County, paralleling the Atlantic Ocean until it empties into Georgetown's Winyah Bay.

The valuable chart also records the principal travel routes. Highway 17 (King's Highway in Horry County) served as the main artery for north-south travel. The Myrtle Beach-Socastee-Conway road opened the door to the west.

Jordan's 1930 map lists estates, early communities and points of historical interest. Some remain, while other names have disappeared from the coastal region.

Below Little River, the following listings appear (north to south): Cherry Grove (H.L. Tilghman) Hog and Cherry Grove Inlet, Ocean Drive, Ward Estate, Windy Hill and Springs Estate.

Next, ARCADY appears in bold print. In the 1920s, the Woodside brothers purchased 66,000 acres of land, including 12 miles of ocean frontage. Their Arcadian dream of an awe-inspiring retreat offering leisure and recreational facilities crashed with the stock market in the Great Depression. The completed Ocean Forest Hotel and Ocean Forest Country Club and Golf Course (now Pine Lakes International Country Club) survived under new ownership.

In 1930, the castle-like ten story hotel, towering 29 feet above sea level, faced the blue Atlantic. People referred to the exquisite structure as the "Million Dollar Hotel." The Ocean Forest Hotel bit the dust on Friday 13, 1974, when the building was demolished.

Myrtle Beach, five miles south of the hotel, was the largest unincorporated village in the country. The coastal resort developed in the center of Long Bay, a sixty-mile stretch of beach between Little River and Georgetown, known today as the Grand Strand.

Withers Swash, two miles south of Myrtle Beach at Spivey's Beach, did not appear on the map. Often it was referred to as Eight Mile Swash, because it extended eight miles from where the Old Kings Highway led onto the strand just north of Singleton Swash.

Next, we find Lewis and Townsend Estates. Adjoining them, Floral Beach, which years later became Surfside Beach.

As we continue south on Jordan's map, we find Vereen and Sparkman Estates, Wachesaw (on the river), Platt's Park and Murrells Inlet. Other listings include: Brookgreen, Magnolia Beach, Wilbrook, Litchfield, Waverly, Caledonia, Pawley's Island, True Blue and Hagley.

I Remember Myrtle Beach When ...

Rounding out the names on the map: Fairfield, Arcadia, Hobcaw, Wheeler Estate (on North Island) and T.A. Yawkey (South Island).

Sixty-seven years have passed since Jordan's map was published. Many changes have occurred, but the Grand Strand (Long Bay) still remains a 60 mile stretch of beautiful sun-swept beach.

DR. J. MARCUS SMITH

During the Depression

The Great Depression crippled Horry County in the early 1930s. By 1935, conditions began to improve when Conway's Paul Quattlebaum, the newly elected State Senator, made a difference. He was a man who could look ahead and plan for the future.

Eight days after taking office, President Franklin D. Roosevelt made the first of his radio "fireside chats." He explained complex issues and the measures being taken to deal with them.

In 1933, the game of Monopoly became a diversion for many people. In a period of economic depression, players enjoyed amassing fortunes and driving opponents bankrupt.

Conditions slowly improved in Horry County. With the organization of C.C.C. (Civilian Conservation Corps), work was begun on building a state park south of Myrtle Beach. The W.P.A. (Works Progress Administration) was also involved in building a dozen schools, gymnasiums, classrooms and streets. It also provided managerial positions.

Margaret Mitchell's 1936 novel, *Gone With The Wind*, portrayed the Old South during the Civil War and Reconstruction. Atlanta rolled out the red carpet for the world movie premier at Loew's Grand Theater on December 15, 1939.

The first week in April 1940, The Palace Theater in Georgetown had the first showing in this area. Afternoon admission was 75 cents. Reserved seats for the evening performances cost $1.10.

The opening of the Intracoastal Waterway in 1936 was a big plus to the economy for Myrtle Beach and Horry County.

In 1936, *Life Magazine* opened a new era of photojournalism. With limited text and photographs on almost every page, it expanded our awareness of current events and the human race. Our Myrtle Beach Sun Fun Festival appeared in the magazine in the early 1950s.

Some changes went almost unnoticed. A bridge replaced the Yauhannah Ferry on the Conway-Georgetown road. In 1935, the Lafayette Bridge was built over the Waccamaw River's southern section, which was the last link in the north-south coastal highway (U.S. 17). In the nation, with much more fanfare, the Golden Gate Bridge in California opened May 28, 1937.

In 1937, *Snow White and the Seven Dwarfs* premiered as this country's first feature-like animated film. The movie classic was comprised of 250,000 separate drawings. The popular motion picture played at Myrtle Beach's Gloria Theater and other area theaters for several days.

The Conway Main Street Memorial Bridge, dedicated to Horry County citizens who served in the armed forces, officially opened April 1, 1938. The elegant concrete bridge over the Waccamaw River replaced the swing bridge on the old two- lane road. For years, it was the only access to the coastal beaches.

With construction cost of $370,000, the tall and stately bridge symbolized a brighter future for Horry County. It was a majestic gateway from the west to the Grand Strand beaches.

DR. J. MARCUS SMITH

Early Myrtle Beach Police Force

In the early 1930s, Myrtle Beach Farms Company built a small one-room brick jail on the southeast corner of Oak Street and 10th Avenue North. Oak trees surrounded the building, and the heavy front door faced 10th Avenue.

The police force consisted of two officers. One served on the day shift and the other had night duty. They worked for Myrtle Beach Farms Company under the supervision of James E. Bryan, Sr.

Gordon S. Beard, Sr., who later became postmaster, served as one of the officers. In later years, residents still called him "Chief Beard."

Old-timers recall when arrests on a big summer weekend crowded the 12 by 12 foot jail. Additional prisoners were handcuffed to the oak trees until they could be transported to the Horry County penal complex in Conway.

Jimmy Miller, a long-time resident, told me that the police officer on duty parked his car by an outside phone booth across the side street from Delta Drug Store, next to Chapin Company. The Myrtle Beach News of June 3, 1937, listed the police headquarters number as 96-J. Anyone who needed help called that number.

Before Myrtle Beach became a municipality on March 12, 1938, it was one of the largest unincorporated villages in the country. The first administration appointed J. F. Hamilton as police chief. Following Hamilton were A. G. Russell, R. S. Weeks and J. M. Stewart. Floyd E. Davis, the fifth chief, served from 1939 until 1947.

In January 1992, Davis made a trip from Bennettsville and attended a special city council meeting. Mayor Bob Grissom presented him with a certificate recognizing him as an honorary citizen of Myrtle Beach.

Davis was known for his innovative use of fingerprint, photographic and investigative techniques. The former chief said "when I came on board departmental equipment consisted mainly of a 'beat-up Ford car.'"

The late Henry H. Bonnette once told me that he first visited Myrtle Beach on July 4, 1935. Bonnette said, "I liked it so much that I moved here and leased the Texaco station near the small depot on the southwest corner of 9th Avenue and Kings Highway in 1936." Bonnette recalled the first temporary City Hall in 1938. He said, "I could look across Kings Highway and see the small structure located between Chapin's Shell Station and the Broadway Restaurant."

In 1940, City Hall, including the police and water department, relocated to the two-story Colonial Building on Kings Highway (the building was demolished in 1992). The new facility occupied the building between the Myrtle Beach Bank and Trust Co. (formerly Myrtle Beach Depository) and the Colonial Drug Store. The drug store housed the bus station office in the rear of the building.

After World War II, growth resumed at a rapid pace. The police and water department moved into their new location on 10th Avenue North in January 1950. A few weeks later, Mayor J. N. Ramsey and the administrative staff moved into the handsome City Hall building, which faced Broadway Extension.

After Chief Davis' resignation, B. W. White, Harry Hunter (acting chief) and Robert L. Lowder headed the police force. W. Carlisle Newton became the city's ninth police chief in May 1949.

Newton was devoted to his wife Eleanor and his profession. Character, reputation and friends were important to him. Eleanor served as my secretary for eight years. We visited often. He once told me,

"After retirement, I'm going to spend more time with my wife. I plan to share with her what time I have left."

After heading the police department for twenty-five years, Chief Newton retired on April 4, 1974 and died September 24, 1976.

J. Stanley Bird spent many years on the force before moving into the top spot in May 1974. Chief Bird implemented many new plans and continued to build the department into a well-organized force. After serving for 17 years, Chief Bird retired in 1991.

After Chief Wayne Player took over the duties for a brief time, Bob Henegar served as interim chief until Sam Killman was installed as the new police chief.

Killman, age 53, retired as Charlotte's police chief in 1991. He left a city with a population of 380,000 for one with 25,000, which swelled to 300,000 during the peak tourist season. Killman came to a 127-member force after overseeing the 1,036-member Charlotte Police Department.

The Myrtle Beach Police Department moved into the modern Law Enforcement Center on Oak Street in October 1982. Before that, the fire department had extended its complex to Oak Street.

Killman retired in March of 1997. City Manager Tom Leath promoted Warren Gall to serve as Myrtle Beach Police Chief.

The little brick jail on the corner of Oak Street and 10th Avenue was demolished. One oak tree remains on the site. It stands as a reminder of Myrtle Beach's early history of a two-man police force and small, one-room jail.

Fire Department

The late Mayor O.C. Calloway was the first fire chief of the town, except for a few months when Charlie Singleton and Eli Saleeby served as day chief and night chief, respectively. The first official firefighting unit on the beach included eighteen volunteer firemen and one fire truck operating from a frame building at the rear of the Broadway Restaurant. From *The Myrtle Beach News:*

The Myrtle Beach Fire Department, an efficiently operating organization, designed to protect the citizens of Myrtle Beach and their property, had its official beginning back in 1936, two years before Myrtle Beach was incorporated.

Except for a few months, O.C. Calloway has served as Fire Chief since the department was organized.

The volunteer group with one fire truck made up the first official firefighting unit here at the beginning.

The station was in a frame building back of the Broadway Restaurant and remained there until the new fire station was completed in 1951.

The department is now operating from two modern buildings and has three engines and two trucks in operation here.

A tribute to the effectiveness of the local department was made Tuesday when it was announced that Myrtle Beach had been awarded a top rating by the Fire Insurance Rating Bureau.

The department now has four full-time men on duty and in addition to the main fire station down town, has another unit on North Kings Highway.

DR. J. MARCUS SMITH

(Probably from the 1955 edition of the paper)

Interview with Jim Callaway (October 13, 1994):

O. C. Callaway worked for S. C. Public Service Authority. He served as Fire Chief, Volunteer, for a small compensation. He began serving in 1938 and stayed with the department until his death in 1954. He died on June 1st, which was during the Sun Fun Festival. The City Hall and Fire Department had black bunting tied to the building. After the death of his father, Jim served as Fire Chief until 1963.

The first fire truck was a Ford, with a dolly engine. Many of the volunteers called it the chuck wagon, because on occasions, it was used as a device to sell hamburgers and hot dogs to raise money for civic purposes.

Number Please

"Number, please," said the operator. I responded, "281-J."

The friendly voice said, "Marcus, the line at Oliver Miller Motors is busy. If you are trying to reach Mrs. Wooten, she's on her way to the Arcade Lunch Room. She'll be walking by your office in a few minutes."

In 1947, the telephone operators added personal touches to their professional services. The 2,500 residents appreciated the family atmosphere of the local company.

Telephone service arrived in Myrtle Beach June 17, 1936. Seacoast Telephone Company installed 25 phones. The directory of the privately owned company occupied two paragraphs on the front page of the weekly *Myrtle Beach News*.

The Lafayette Manor, near 9th Avenue North and Chester Street, housed the one-room office. Sammy Norton and his daughter operated the switchboard for several years. In 1939, the equipment was moved to a three-bedroom cottage between 9th and 10th Avenues on Chester Street.

In 1941, the directory listed 90 subscribers. The late Mabel Fleming became the manager and chief operator. Her daughters, Evon and Marion, assisted their mother. The company paid them a total of $100 per month and provided living quarters.

Late night calls were mainly for taxi service. The girls shared a double bed in a room adjacent to the office. The one nearest the switchboard responded to the first call. They traded places in the bed and the other sister took the next call.

While operating the switchboard, Marion's frequent conversations with H. P. Martin brought about a summer wedding in 1942.

DR. J. MARCUS SMITH

In the mid-1940s, the beach was a small town. Phone repair service was available only on Mondays, according to Evon (Mrs. Alton Benton). A repairman would travel from Georgetown to service the local phones. The telephone operator provided an answering and information center. Typical of the requests: "If I get any calls, I'll be at Chapin's." "Where's my Mama?" "What's on at the picture show?" "What time is it?"

The Georgetown office handled in-state long distance calls. The Marion office completed out-of-state service. In 1948, Myrtle Beach became a toll center, and local operators completed all long distance calls. The local exchange had grown to three local operating and three long-distance toll positions.

Evon made the first long distance call from Myrtle Beach in June 1948---to Pueblo, Colorado. She said, "I reached an operator in Florence, then connected to Charlotte, then to Chicago, then Denver and finally Pueblo. It took about five minutes.

Dial service was established in 1951. By 1952, the long distance traffic required six operating toll positions. At this time there were approximately 500 phones in service and twelve girls were employed as long distance operators.

General Telephone purchased Seacoast Telephone in 1957. It began service to the coastal area from the North Carolina line to Georgetown and west to Conway. By August 1965, more than 12,000 numbers were listed in the directory.

Horry Telephone Cooperative was established in June 1952, with 214 customers, which increased to 421 in 1954.

On December 12, 1986, the Myrtle Beach toll center closed. Evon was invited back to make the last call. She said, "I plugged into the telephone line. The caller wanted to place a credit card call." She keyed in the number, pushed a button and the transaction was over in 30 seconds. After 38 years, no more long distance calls would be handled at Myrtle Beach.

In June 1991, GTE listed over 54,000 access lines from the North Carolina line to the far side of Surfside Beach and Conway. Horry Telephone Cooperative served a large section and listed approximately 45,000 access lines.

Seacoast Telephone served its purpose in the history of Myrtle Beach. The first office building, now a residence, was moved to nearby Withers Drive. The walls of the white frame house no longer echo the friendly voice of the operator saying, "Number, please."

DR. J. MARCUS SMITH

Mayors of Myrtle Beach

In the Myrtle Beach Township in 1937, petitions were circulated for signatures requesting the Secretary of State to issue a charter for incorporation.

The proposed corporate limits extended north of the Ocean Forest Hotel (at the foot of Poinsett Road) and stretched to the northern boundary of Myrtle Beach State Park to the south -- a distance of ten miles along the ocean front, with a depth of about half a mile.

Voters approved the incorporation of Myrtle Beach, with 137 favorable votes and eight against the proposal. The first municipal (mayor-council) election was scheduled for 1938.

Sixty-eight years later, on January 11, 2006, John T. Rhodes became the thirteenth Mayor of Myrtle Beach. Judge Jennifer Wilson performed the ceremony at the Ted C. Collins Law Enforcement Center at 1101 N. Oak Street in Myrtle Beach.

In the 1938 election, Dr. W. LeRoy Harrelson, a pharmacist, defeated J. N. Ramsey, president and general manager of the Nu Way Laundry, by 11 votes, 74-63, to become the first mayor. Six Council members elected were: R.H. Cannon, Sr. with 135 votes followed by B.B. Benfield (132), William "Bill" Rourk, MD (131), J.C. Macklen (128), A.P. Shirley (128) and R.M. Hussey, Jr. (101).

In the next election, Ben M. Graham narrowly defeated the incumbent Harrelson. Graham served one term and lost to Harrelson in the following election.

O.C. Calloway served two terms as Myrtle Beach's third mayor (1943-1947). Calloway also headed the local fire department.

During the administration of Harry W. Tallevast (l947-1949), Councilman Dr. Bill Rourk died and Dr. Waldo H. Jones was appointed to complete his term.

After an earlier attempt for the mayor's post, J.N. Ramsey successfully became the fifth mayor in 1949 and served two terms until 1954. During his administration, the present City Hall was completed and the executive offices were moved into the new facility.

Ernest W. Williams took office in January 1954. Williams will be remembered for his guidance and direction when Hurricane Hazel slammed into the coastal area on October 15, 1954. Williams died in office in 1955. The council elected mayor pro-tem W.E. Cameron to fill the vacancy. Mark C. Garner was named mayor pro-tem, to take Cameron's place.

After Colonel Cameron served as mayor for the remainder of William's administration, he was reelected to two terms (1958-1966). Robert Grissom acted as mayor pro-tem (1963-65).

Mark C. Garner, former owner and publisher of *The Sun-News*, directed the local government for eight years as its eighth mayor.

Mayor Robert J. Hirsch served from 1974-1978. The next Mayor was Erick C. Ficken, who served two terms (1978-1986).

Robert M. (Bob) Grissom was elected and served three terms (1986-1998) as Myrtle Beach's eleventh mayor, the longest tenure (12 years) of any elected official in the history of Myrtle Beach.

On January 6, 1998 Mark Struthers McBride (1998-2006) was sworn in as the twelfth and youngest Mayor of Myrtle Beach. David Harwell, retired Chief Justice, administered the oath of office.

DR. J. MARCUS SMITH

Old Beach Road

Prior to the opening of the Conway Main Street Memorial Bridge over the Waccamaw River in 1938, traveling to Myrtle Beach proved to be a tiresome journey. The long, winding 21-mile road from Conway to Myrtle Beach by way of Socastee had 33 curves.

Philip Thompson, former Conway Mayor, and I recently shared some time together. We toured the Conway area and talked about our pre-teen years. In those days, we had to depend on our parents, relatives or older friends for transportation to the beach.

In the mid-l930s, summer traffic from the west traveled through Marion, Aynor, Cool Spring and Homewood before arriving in Conway. Beach-bound tourists, along with locals, traveled down Main Street to 3rd Avenue and made a left turn at the Town Hall. After one block, motorists turned right at Kingston Presbyterian Church, and one hundred yards away, a left turn at Quattlebaum's Light and Ice Company.

Long-time residents remember the noisy wooden-plank bridge across the mouth of Kingston Lake, which was the next step on the road to Myrtle Beach. Air-conditioning did not exist and people slept with their windows open. In the still of hot summer nights, the bump-bump-bump sound of automobile tires crossing the loose boards in the bridge echoed throughout the town as tourists headed for the beach.

LaRue (Bud) Langston, whose parent's house faced the bridge, said, "I spent many restless nights counting the bumps as cars traveled to the coast." Langston also recalled that when a freshet occurred, water covered the road and the base of the magnolia tree in their front yard.

The bridge no longer exists, so Thompson and I crossed the lake on the Highway 905 concrete bridge and walked to the other side of the former Kingston Lake Bridge. From there, we followed the old route a short distance and observed the curve of the old road as it approached the Waccamaw River.

We located the site where the drawbridge, which was built prior to 1920, once stood. The bridge had crossed at the narrowest part of the river, which had high banks on both sides. As we observed some remaining pilings, we saw the nearby trestle bridge, which still stands at the original site of the early train route.

In order to trace the old roadway on the east side of the river, Thompson and I crossed the high-rise Main Street Bridge and exited to the left. A few hundred yards away, we parked at a clearing in the woods and walked west towards the river on the old worn-and-broken hard surfaced road.

The original narrow roadway rambled through swampy land until it brought us to a gorge full of river water that contained many pilings from one of the two wooden bridges leading from the old drawbridge. High water often covered the many low-lying bridges.

On the old road, we crossed the railroad tracks and continued our drive towards Myrtle Beach. On the left, Thompson pointed out where O.L. Williams Veneer Mfg. plant once stood. The company produced plywood for the Williams Furniture Company in Sumter.

As we continued, we crossed the tracks again and on our left was the Stilley Mill, which also produced plywood. Four generations of Stilleys from Conway have operated the mill.

We crossed another low-lying bridge, which is now concrete, as we approached the Red Hill section, near the third set of train tracks. Looking beyond the busy Highway 501, we saw the old route to Myrtle Beach, which today is Highway 544.

The old road curved to the left in Socastee and continued for nine miles entering downtown Myrtle Beach on today's Highway 15.

Eason's Store at Murrells Inlet

In the late 1930s, my parents occasionally traveled to Murrells Inlet. The highlight of the journey was a stop at Eason's country store near the Inlet. They enjoyed visiting with Captain James Alton Eason, Sr. My first cousin, Edward Smith, often accompanied us on the trip.

After leaving Conway, we crossed Kingston Lake Bridge and the swing bridge over the Waccamaw River. The bituminous surfaced road led to Red Hill and on to Socastee (Highway 544). At the junction, the paved road went to Myrtle Beach. On the right, the narrow road (707) continued to Murrells Inlet.

My father drove the black Ford along the sandy-rutted road. When we met a car, he put our left wheels in the right rut and the passing car used the other furrow. The road was paved in 1942.

Road 707 continued to the main thoroughfare at the Inlet. After we passed Collins Creek Baptist Church, we usually turned right on River Road (known as Journey's End). At Wachesaw Road, we turned left and traveled east to Eason's Country Store, a short distance from the creek.

Recently Hazel Hatchell and I visited Jack and Danny Eason at the Gasoline Alley Convenience store at the corner of Wachesaw Road and Highway 17 By-Pass. Hatchell had attended grade school with them.

As Danny waited on customers, Jack shared with us the store's history. Captain Eason migrated from Snow Hill, N.C. to the Willow Springs section of Horry County. John Eason, his father, settled in Murrells Inlet. Later Captain Eason moved his family to the Inlet in 1918, and he and his oldest son, Edwin, opened the store. Other sons were Jimmy, Eric, Eugene and two daughters, Louise and Leona. Jack and Danny are Edwin's sons.

DR. J. MARCUS SMITH

Rocking chairs lined the wide front porch. Inside the store, a potbellied stove stood near the long counter. A beverage box was located at the other end. Orange Crush, Nehi and R.C. cola filled the chest. They sold dry goods, hardware and over-the-counter drugs. All types of seafood were available.

Their truck farm supplied the locals with fresh produce. After Sandy Island residents made their purchases, Capt. Eason offered free delivery to their boats down Wachesaw Road to the Waccamaw River.

The Easons lived in a two-story frame house diagonally across from the store. Captain Eason died in 1957. Edwin continued to operate the store, until a tragic truck accident took his life in October 1963. His sons Jack and Danny and a daughter survive Edwin's first marriage and six sons and two daughters by the second.

While Hatchell and I conversed with the Eason boys, Danny looked through the large glass window and pointed to the middle of the Highway 17 By-Pass. He said, "That's where the old store once stood."

From his book, *Musings of a Hermit*, the closing lines of the late Clarke Willcox's poem, <u>De Ole Sto'</u>, written in 1965, sums up the swan song of Eason's Store.

> "Dey gwine to tear de ole sto' down, uproot de live oak trees,
> For thru' here go a four-lane road. Dey'll pass us lak a breeze.
> Dis place gwine be a mem'ry uv easy-goin' days;
> Dey change de look uv ebryting, dey even change our ways.
> Perhaps I'll take a picture so folk will kno' it's so,
> Dat where dey speeds at seventy, dere stood a country sto'."

Myrtle Beach's First Football Team

In 1930, the first Myrtle Beach High School diplomas were awarded to six local students. Classes were held in the grammar school building which faced Oak Street between 5th and 6th Avenues North. Prior to that time, students completed their secondary education in Conway. Several years later, the county built the two-story high school section, which joined the elementary school and overlooked Kings Highway. The school complex burned in 1946.

Members of the 1938 Myrtle Beach High School football squad, the school's first team ever, celebrated with classmates at their 45th homecoming October 28, 1983.

Prior to the Myrtle Beach-Bennettsville game, the attending players met at a local restaurant for a pre-game meal. They were: Dewey Nye, Orson Bone, Grady West, John Harris, Dewey Bell, Chester Todd, Roy Harrelson, Earl Huggins, Edwin Bone, Andre Garr, Jack Jordan, Holmes Springs, David Springs and Coach Ernie Southern.

Superintendent L. N. Clark coached the thirty young men on the initial football team. Principal Ernie Southern served as assistant coach. Dr. Bill Rourk, a local physician, took care of their medical needs, while David Springs, Class of '41, was appointed the team manager.

The squad practiced on a sand-spur-laden grassland at the corner of Oak Street and 12th Avenue North, which later became the site of the first football field.

Dr. Holmes Springs recalled they played four games the first year: Loris, Conway, Hemingway and Marion. The events were scheduled on the opponent's field until adequate improvements were made locally.

David Springs said, "The following year home games were played off 10th Avenue N. on George Trask Farms. The football field was located at one end of a makeshift run-way that catered to small local planes. Many fans brought their own chairs and sat by the large drainage ditches that eventually emptied into Withers Swash."

Earl Huggins quarter-backed the first team. He said, "When I showed up for work battered and bruised on Saturday morning at the A & P Store, Manager A. P. Shirley thought I had been in a fist fight." Years later, Huggins served as head football coach at Myrtle Beach High School.

Roy Harrelson said, "During our first game a crushing tackle left me sprawling. Dr. Rourk observed that one of my fingers was bent, but I re-entered the game. Today, that same finger is still crooked."

The student body staged a contest to select a name for the school's mascot. Many names were submitted, but only two were approved by the students. The late John Harris withdrew his proposal, because he preferred Sarah Jackson Southern's entry "Seahawks." The name still stands today.

After the completion of the Myrtle Beach Memorial Stadium in 1968, the Seahawks scheduled their home games on the new playing surface. The modern facility is still located on 33rd Avenue N. in the midst of Myrtle Beach's School Complex.

At the first home football game in 1994, the city renamed the facility "Doug Shaw Memorial Stadium," in memory of the long-time and successful football coach of Myrtle Beach High School.

Yaupon Swash

In the 1930s, the area became known as Spivey's Beach. Joe Sarkis' fish shack occupied the only site on the oceanfront. Sarkis' fishing boats came ashore there, and he sold his fish locally and in his Conway Fish Market.

Slightly south of the pavilion was Withers Swash. The entrance to the swash was just south of 3rd Avenue South and wandered up and down the beach with changes in tides and seasons. The swash waters extended south for several blocks, between the large sand dunes and front row lots.

The larger tidal waters flowed west, curving and flowing under a wooden bridge at a popular swimming hole, Yaupon Swash. The water continued beneath another narrow bridge on Kings Highway and into Withers Lake, which is now located behind Walgreen's at the corner of 3rd Avenue South and Kings Highway, and bounded by 5th Avenue South and Charlotte Road.

In the early 1940's, the entrance to the swash was dug out and sea walls were erected on either side of the Withers Swash entrance to keep the channel flowing in one direction. A wooden walkover bridge was constructed, which allowed people to walk the length of the beach at high tide.

The swash was a clean, beautiful tidal creek and lake. We learned to swim in the clear salty water. The area teemed with fish, shrimp and crabs.

The following comments are from various interviews with Tempe Oehler, B.M. Spivey and Francis McCormick:

Withers Swash is near Spivey's Beach and Spivey's Swash, located beside the present Holiday Inn Downtown, former site of the USO building during World War II. Mr. Hughes engineered the first retaining walls for the swash there and did an educated study of the ebb and flow and course of the tide before erecting those walls.

Abundance of Yaupon bushes. Large Oak tree, with rope on large limb, enables swimmers to swing out over Yaupon Swash..............The ole' swimming hole, on high tide.

Nye's Drug Stores

On June 8, 1991, Mary Joyce Hosse Nye, wife of David Sherwood (Jimmy) Nye, Jr., of Conway, was a patient at Richland Memorial Hospital in Columbia. I spoke with her on the phone that afternoon to express my concern about her heart condition. After a brief conversation, she said, "Marcus, please write an article for me on Nye's Drug Store?" Mary Joyce died early in the morning on the 10th.

Mary Joyce met Jimmy Nye in the Main Street Pharmacy, when she came to Conway to teach. They were married June 16, 1949. She taught math, science, and art in the Conway Public Schools for twenty years.

Of the four Nye Brothers, Jimmy and R. Bruce migrated to Conway in the late 1920s. Jimmy had served with the chain of Wiggins Drug Stores in N.C., while Bruce had worked at the Palace Drug Store in Mullins for ten years.

In 1928, the train tracks were removed from downtown Main Street in Conway. The same year an announcement appeared in the *Horry Herald* which stated: "On Friday, June 22, we are extending an invitation to everyone to attend the opening of Nye's Drug Store on Main Street. The very newest things in drug store merchandise from all over the world are brought together in one place. You can get anything you want from early morning till late at night."

People flocked to Nye's Pharmacy for the opening day festivities. With smiling faces the experienced staff, Chapman Thompson and George Bacot, greeted the overflow crowd and presented them with free gifts and ice cream.

DR. J. MARCUS SMITH

On January 15, 1937, Dewey F. Nye opened Nye's Drug Store in Myrtle Beach (across from Chapin Company). Several years later, George L. Nye started Nye's Pharmacy in Mullins.

In the late 1930s and early 1940s, Conway teenagers used bicycles and roller skates, or walked. A few had automobiles. The high school was located a mile from downtown, and after school students crowded the soda fountain at Nye's, one of the popular hangouts. Voices filled the air with orders of a coke with a lemon twist, a grape drink, or a cherry coke. Some even skated into the store and relaxed in one of the many booths and ate boiled peanuts, which were five-cents a bag.

Many people in town enjoyed the services of Nye's. Telephone number 98 was for home orders. Boys on bicycles delivered the items, with no tipping allowed. Curb service proved to be a big success. With a beep of a car horn, boy curb hops responded to the call.

E.O. (Buddy) Watson worked at Nye's for several years. Recently, he told me, "I made $5 per week, with five cents withheld for social security. After school, I worked from 3:15 p.m. until 7 p.m. one day, and until 11 p.m. the next day. Saturday was a full day, but I was off every other Sunday."

Watson also mentioned behind-the-fountain lingo. He said, "Number one meant throw me a towel, number 81, the code for a glass of water. Number 84 denoted four glasses of water."

In June 1953, Nye's opened a branch pharmacy near the old Conway Hospital on 9th Avenue, and Jimmy Nye moved to the new location. He retired in May 1992.

At that time, Nye's Drug Store in Myrtle Beach catered to the needs of locals and tourists. John Singleton started waiting on tables and later jerking sodas at the age of nine. Singleton said, "Dewey and Myrtle Nye encouraged me to enter Pharmacy College after I graduated from Myrtle Beach High School in l950." Myrtle Beach Nye's closed in the late 1950s and reopened under a new name and ownership.

Both Nye's stores continued to flourish in Conway, but eventually the Main Street Nye's closed in 1970. The store held wonderful memories for many people.

When I visit my parents' graves in Lakeside Cemetery, I always walk a few yards to the Nye Plot. As I pay my respects, I think of Mary Joyce, a devoted wife and mother, a teacher, a friend of all, and a lover of Nye's Drug Store.

DR. J. MARCUS SMITH

Post Office

A plaque on the inside wall of the Myrtle Beach Post Office reads: "This building dedicated to Public Service in 1982. Ronald Reagan, President of the United States and William F. Bolger, Postmaster General." The modern building is another step in the history of the resort city's postal facilities.

At the turn of the century, Burroughs and Collins Co. had established many lumber camps in the area. They built a General Store on Ninth Avenue, between the present Oak Street and Kings Highway, to serve the local community.

Myrtle Beach's first Post Office, which opened May 21, 1901, was housed in the back of the General Store. George R. Sessions served as the first postmaster until 1902, after which John McNeill assumed the duties.

James H. Marsh became postmaster in May, 1905 and was followed by J. Waterman Cook (1906), Jerry B. Cox (1908), George W. Booth (1911), John W. Arnold (1912), James E. Bryan, Sr. (1912) and George C. Cox. (1915)

Recently, I visited Harold Clardy, President of Chapin Company. He showed me an official document signed by Harry S. New, Postmaster General, March 24, 1926, which certified Grover C. Graham as postmaster. He was the last one to serve in the first post office.

In 1928, the post office relocated to the modern Chapin Building, and George C. Cox assumed the post again on Valentine's Day. After his retirement, Mrs. Lillian Caldwell served as acting postmaster for one year.

Gordon S. Beard became postmaster on July 2, 1932. His one regular clerk, Nell Lucas Outlaw, received a salary of $30.00 per month. Verona Clardy (Mrs. John Swartz) served as a summer clerk and received the same salary. Other early employees were Arlan Cooper, Maude White and Thelma Martin.

Clardy showed me a 1939 picture of Chapin Company that hangs in his office. The post office occupied an area, 25 feet wide and 25 feet deep, between Delta Drug Store and Chapin's Department Store on Broadway (now Main Street).

Horry Benton, long-time resident, said, "In the late 1920s, I worked for the Ocean Forest Country Club (now Pine Lakes International Countrry Club). Every day I picked up their mail at the post office." Benton added, "When you entered the small post office, a door to the left went into Delta Drug Store. To the right, a door led to Chapin Department Store. A few mail boxes graced the wall on either side of the postal window. At night, the two side doors were locked."

During those early years, people would gather at the post office, Delta Drug Store and Chapin's waiting for the incoming mail to be processed. Myrtle Beach's only physician, Dr. Bill Rourk, occupied an office next to the drug store. He often relieved Postmaster Beard during the lunch hour.

Myrtle Beach Farms Company built additions to their Chapin complex and leased a large area to the government for a new post office. In February 1941, Myrtle Beach had its first separate facility to house the post office.

Gordon S. Beard continued to serve as postmaster. Former employees have told me they jokingly commented that his middle initial stood for "Stamps."

Beard retired as postmaster March 31, 1953. W. M. Stackhouse, Jr. succeeded him and served until April 14, 1954. F. C. Hammond was acting postmaster briefly until H. K. Sanders took office on May 1, 1955.

When the post office outgrew its facility, it moved into a new modern building on the corner of 10th Avenue and Oak Street, in June 1963. Sanders died on March 24, 1965 and S. L. Davis became acting postmaster June 19, 1965. John H. Atkinson, Jr. was sworn in as postmaster in 1966 at the Oak Street location and continued his duties when the present post office was dedicated in 1982.

After Atkinson retired, W. Richard Bowers assumed the duties of postmaster November 21, 1987.

In 1930, the post office recorded $5,078 in postal receipts. A total of $330,590 was reported in 1965. Bowers said "1994 should top $14,000,000.

Myrtle Beach Newspapers

The first newspapers established in Horry County were *The Horry Dispatch* (1861) and *The Telephone* (1878). In 1886, The *Conway Horry Herald* began publication, which was followed by *The Conway Field* in 1902. Myrtle Beach newspapers began in the late 1920s.

The late Henry Trezevant (Trez) Willcox moved from Marion, S.C. in 1926 and became secretary and "general office man" for John T. Woodside. The Woodside Brothers had ambitious and extensive plans for the development of Myrtle Beach.

The promotion of the coastal hamlet became an obsession with Willcox, and he immediately started writing articles (mostly news items) about Myrtle Beach. The articles were relayed to Greenville, Spartanburg, Charleston and other daily papers.

Charming News of Charming Myrtle Beach, the first news sheet, appeared in 1927. Willcox distributed the mimeographed bulletin to local residents.

The Myrtle Beach Leaf replaced the first publication. William P. Jacobs printed and illustrated the material in the monthly news leaflet. Willcox prepared and edited the articles.

J. Clarence Macklen established a mercantile business in Myrtle Beach in 1926. The venture proved successful, and he moved into the downtown area at the junction of Broadway and the present Highway 501.

In the back of the wooden store, Macklen and his brother-in-law, Claude L. Phillips, started Myrtle Beach's first print shop. Their office had one job press, a small paper cutter and a limited supply of type.

Phillips did all the commercial work. Later they purchased a small press and more type and created a small weekly paper.

The first issue of *The Myrtle Beach News*, reported to be the oldest tabloid newspaper in South Carolina, went to press in June of l935. The publication developed into a standard size weekly paper in 1939.

In 1946, W. A. Kimbel, who lived at Wachesaw Plantation near Murrells Inlet, bought *The Myrtle Beach News*. After a brief tenure in the newspaper business, Kimbel received a call from Washington requesting him to serve the government in Europe as field administrator of the Marshall Plan.

In 1949 Kimbel sold the paper to James Lee Platt, owner and publisher of *The Mullins Enterprise*. After several successful years as Editor of the *Myrtle Beach News*, Platt sold the paper to W. L. Harrelson, Jr. in 1954.

Eventually, Harrelson converted the paper into a semi-weekly. Later, the *Myrtle Beach News* operated for a while as the only daily paper in South Carolina's upper coastal region.

When Harrelson accepted the position as press secretary to former Governor Ernest F. Hollings (now U.S. Senator), he sold the paper to Chicora Publishing Company, which after a few months sold it to the Grand Strand Publishing Company.

In 1961, the late Mark Garner, owner and publisher of *The Sun*, a weekly local paper, merged with the bi-weekly *Myrtle Beach News*. Garner said, "For the present the combined *Sun-News* will be published on Wednesdays."

In 1962, the paper went bi-weekly, on Thursday and Saturday. In 1972, editions of the *Sun-News* were published on Tuesday, Thursday and Saturday with a circulation of 6,600.

The State Record Co. acquired the *Sun-News* in 1973. The hyphen was eliminated, and the paper began publishing Monday through Saturday with all subscriptions by mail. The Sunday edition was added in 1977.

Knight-Ridder Inc. bought The Sun Publishing Co. and other properties of The State-Record Co. in 1986. The average Sunday circulation hit a record high of 35,191.

The first major change, a complete redesign, occurred in 1988. Lots of color was added, George the mascot got a new look and typefaces were changed.

Sixty-seven years have passed since the humble beginning of the newspaper in Myrtle Beach. In 1994, approximately 44,000 copies of *The Sun News* roll off the press on Sunday and about 37,000 papers are published during the week.

DR. J. MARCUS SMITH

Rourk Brothers

On a June afternoon, the heat hovered around the two-story white colonial house of Dr. Henderson Rourk in Shallotte, N.C. Dr. Rourk and I visited in the comfort of his air-conditioned home and talked of his approaching 90th birthday.

Dr. William Asbury (Bill) Rourk, Jr. and Dr. Malcolm H. (Henderson) Rourk were born in Wilmington in 1898 and 1903.

In 1927, Dr. Bill Rourk opened his office in Myrtle Beach in a small frame house on the corner of 7th Avenue North and Kings Highway. After Chapin Company opened in 1928, he moved into office space provided for him next to Delta Drug Store.

The late Elfreida Singleton often talked with me about those early years. "Dr. Bill attended my late husband's father in the country. He would make visits any hour of the day or night. Dr. Bill was a blessing to all of us. We have some great doctors on the Grand Strand, but we will never, never have another Dr. Bill Rourk."

After practicing several years in Shallotte, Henderson Rourk joined his brother in Myrtle Beach in 1939.

Margie Nance Benton spoke most highly of Dr. Henderson Rourk. She said, "One morning in 1940, I returned from the clothesline and discovered that my infant son's face had turned blue. I immediately contacted Dr. Rourk. He came at once. He diagnosed a malfunctioning heart valve." Dr. Rourk traveled with Margie and her husband, Eddie, to the Conway Hospital. Dr. Archie Sasser, Conway surgeon, assisted in the successful treatment.

I Remember Myrtle Beach When ...

During World War II, Dr. Henderson Rourk volunteered and served with the Army Medical Corps for several years, then returned to Myrtle Beach in 1946.

Due to declining health of his parents, he returned to his native home in Shallotte in 1947. He later purchased the Forrest Building in Myrtle Beach. During the 20 years I rented from him, we developed a strong friendship.

Bill Rourk, often called "Dr. Bill," became a tremendous influence in the beach community.

Apart from his medical duties, he served as treasurer and deacon of the Presbyterian Church and on the local school board. Besides being a Mason and Rotarian, he occupied a seat on the first City Council when Myrtle Beach was incorporated in 1938.

Bill Rourk and his wife "Mac" became the parents of two sons, William A. III and James "Roddy" Rodman Rourk. When I opened my office in 1947, Bill Rourk was among the first to welcome me to Myrtle Beach. His outgoing and sincere personality made that first impression permanent.

At age 50, Dr. Bill suffered a heart attack. He died two weeks later at his home on May 18, 1948.

Roddy Rourk continued to represent the family by serving the community as a local school administrator, outstanding high school math teacher, active Methodist Church member and Boy Scout leader. Roddy died Dec. 23, 1984.

The 1993 June visit with Dr. Henderson Rourk, now deceased, brought back memories of early days in Myrtle Beach, when life moved at a slower pace.

DR. J. MARCUS SMITH

It's A Girl

Dr. William "Bill" Rourk, an early Myrtle Beach physician, emerged from a room on the first floor of the Ocean Forest Hotel. As Horry Benton paced the long hall, the weary doctor approached him and said, "It's a girl. Lucille is fine." Their first born, Claudia Elizabeth, arrived on Saturday, March 25, 1933.

Everette Horry Benton, a son of Edward and Elizabeth Ellis Benton, was born in Horry County. The other children were born in Brunswick County, N.C.

Even though Benton was born in Myrtle Beach on July 18, 1913, he spent his early years in the Hickory Grove section (outside of Conway) near the present Highway 905. At an early age, he joined two of his brothers on a construction job at the Ocean Forest Country Club, later renamed the Pine Lakes International Country Club.

Benton said, "My job consisted of digging stumps, shoveling dirt and helping prepare the first nine fairways. With an oat seeder, I drove the mules and scattered the first grass seeds on the golf course."

After the golf course opened, Benton returned to Hickory Grove and assisted his sister on the farm for a season. The following year, he moved on the farm of the Perry Hardees. Benton fell in love with their daughter, Lucille, and they married on January 2, 1932.

Benton said, "After we married, we needed a stove. We visited the Kingston Furniture Store (fore runner of Goldfinch Funeral Home) on Main Street in Conway. We informed the owner, W.M. (Will) Goldfinch, that we did not have any money. Mr. Will remembered my father. He provided funeral services for my mother in 1919. He told us to pick out a stove, and we could pay for it after tobacco season."

On our two acres of tobacco, heavy rains ruined the crop. After being cured, the tobacco sold for trash. Benton said, "Our income for the year was a little corn, sweet potatoes and $15. We paid Mr. Goldfinch $7 for the little four-eyed stove. Our farming career ended. We moved back to the beach. I started working again at the golf course. For a while, we lived in a 20 foot by 20 foot room, with a fireplace, on the grounds."

In 1933, the bankrupt Ocean Forest Hotel had to be guarded for insurance purposes. Mr. Robert White, golf course architect and designer of the country club, served as custodian of the properties. He asked the Bentons to stay in the hotel. They were offered two nice bedrooms with kitchen privileges. Water and lights were included. The salary was $28 per month. Benton continued his work at the golf course.

Later, Mr. White informed the Bentons that the hotel would soon open again. They moved, but the Grand Strand became their permanent home.

Today, Horry and Lucille Benton still recall that day in March of 1933, when they were the sole occupants of the Ocean Forest Hotel, and Dr. Bill Rourk walked down the lonesome hall saying "It's a girl."

Patricia Inn

Patricia Inn in the 1950s
(Photo courtesy of Jack Thompson – All Rights Reserved)

The fashionable Patricia, 102 rooms in three buildings, faced the blue Atlantic Ocean. The well-liked Inn was located on a 500 foot site at 28th Avenue on North Ocean Boulevard.

The startling news of the forthcoming destruction of The Patricia spread like wildfire on the Grand Strand and throughout the Carolinas. The walls of the well-known landmark came tumbling down in 1985 to make way for The Patricia Grande.

In the midst of The Great Depression, a young Patricia Forester Rousseau and her family left their North Wilkesboro home in the North Carolina Mountains and headed to the South Carolina coast in 1934.

In a 1985 *Sun News* interview, the late Patricia Boyd recalled those early years. "Only a scattering of boarding homes and cottages lined the beach. Larger hotels for families did not exist. I wanted a family place, that's what we built. The magnificent Ocean Forest Hotel stood at the north end of the beach, but its city-style elegance didn't offer a homey atmosphere."

The original Patricia, Patricia Court, was built on the south end of the property. Josephine Forester, of Myrtle Beach, said, "I met my husband, the late J. Herbert Forester, who worked at the Patricia." Herb assisted Patricia, his older sister, in the early years. The Patricia Inn followed in 1941. Later, The Patricia Seaside Apartments on the north end of the lot completed the complex.

The three-story Patricia Inn became the centerpiece of the popular retreat, a home away from home. The striking white building, with green and white awnings, appeared to stand guard over the ocean and wide surf-smoothed beach. In the early morning, beach chairs and umbrellas were positioned in the sun-bleached sand for guests of The Patricia. Rocking chairs lined the front porch patio. The lobby and dining room were reminiscent of days gone by, with columns and elaborate molding. A hand-carved hand-rail extended to the third floor.

In 1954, Hurricane Hazel damaged the Inn and Court. A new structure replaced The Patricia Court. After the Inn received a face-lift, a spacious sprawling lobby and enlarged dining room greeted the faithful guests.

In the 1985 interview, Patricia Boyd said, "My partner and former husband, Joe Ivey, sold the facility in the late 1970s to Myrtle Beach investors."

Gayle P. Floyd, manager of the Patricia from 1970 to 1985 said, "The trend in Myrtle Beach is changing. Not everybody wants what we offer. There's a younger generation that wants something different."

DR. J. MARCUS SMITH

After 51 years, The Patricia's quiet, simple and uneventful nature of old southern charm went out with the tide. The incoming surge promises elaborate high-rise condominiums for a new generation.

Ocean Plaza Hotel

In 1922, a group of business and professional men from Conway and throughout the Pee Dee built the Yacht Club on the ocean front at 14th Avenue North in Myrtle Beach.

A clay-sand road led from the pavilion area to the three-story modern building, which included the coastal area's first fishing pier.

An increasing number of vehicles were appearing on the scene, and sidewalks did not show up until the late 1930s. A wooden boardwalk on the beach was a welcome addition for the 200 local residents and growing number of summer tourists.

The late Sam P. Gardner bought the Yacht Club in the mid-thirties. Gardner, a school teacher and devoted Methodist, disliked the implication of the "Club" label. Later, he renamed the stately structure, Ocean Plaza Hotel.

The Hotel, which served three meals daily, immediately became a popular place for tourists during the summer season. The 30 foot wide pier offered the best fishing along the coast. When the spots and whitings were running, news spread like wildfire, and locals scampered to join other fishermen.

On a weekend, our family and friends spent endless hours on the pier. At the end of a day, we often had two or three large tubs of fish. We spent the evening sharing our catch with neighbors and friends.

In October of 1946, Gardner announced the completion of the remodeling and extension of the pier. The overall addition of 300 feet made the pier 925 feet long.

In 1950, Gardner made extensive renovations on the interior and exterior of the hotel. The following year, he leased the Ocean Plaza

Hotel to the late George M. Hendrix. Gardner continued to devote full time to the fishing pier, which was excluded from the lease.

According to the April 27, 1951 edition of the *Myrtle Beach News*, Hendrix said, "We will continue to operate the hotel dining room. The Marine Room, on ground level, will open in May." The lounge consisted of a dance floor, juke box and soda fountain, which served light refreshments. Fishermen, along with locals, enjoyed the refreshing sea breezes which drifted through open arch ways in the facility.

Captain Sam Gardner's boat, *The Carolina Queen*, docked at Vereen's Marina. When weather permitted, passengers boarded at the end of the Ocean Plaza Pier.

Gardner's brother-in-law Bill Copeland assisted in the operation of the 83-foot cruiser. They offered deep-sea fishing trips from 8 a.m. to 4 p.m., daily except Sunday. Pleasure excursions were from 8 to 10 p.m. Sunday sight-seeing excursions were scheduled from 3 to 6 p.m. The charge for night and Sunday cruises was two dollars.

Frances Hendrix Smith said, "I recall boarding the boat at the end of the pier and taking a pleasure cruise up and down the coast."

Smith also said, "After Hendrix operated the Ocean Plaza Hotel for several years, my brother, the late Edgar A. Blume, assumed the lease and managed the Hotel for ten years."

In the 1960s, Gardner sold the Ocean Plaza Hotel and Fishing Pier to a group of Grand Strand businessmen. The corporation had the building demolished, and they built the Yachtsman Hotel on the site. They completed the north tower in 1971 and the south tower in 1972.

A fishing pier still stands at the original site. It serves as a reminder of the early days in Myrtle Beach when the Yacht Club and Ocean Plaza Hotel faced the pier.

Archibald Rutledge

As I dusted books in my modest library, my eyes focused on a small hard-back publication, *Veiled Eros.* The author, Archibald Rutledge, had presented my parents with his autographed book of poems, one of many, in 1938.

My family operated The S.C. Plant and Seed Company in Conway. Rutledge often visited their store and purchased azaleas and other plants for Hampton Plantation. As a pre-teen, I worked in the nursery during the busy season. One afternoon as I helped load azaleas in his truck, I met the distinguished gentleman.

Archibald Rutledge was born October 23, 1883 in the "Summer Place," along Jeremy Creek, in McClellanville, S. C. His father built the log house about 1870 in the region known as The Village.

Several weeks after his birth, his parents returned to the plantation at Hampton, 10 miles from McClellanville and 15 miles southwest of Georgetown. For many years the plantation, an 18th- century Georgian mansion, was his actual residence.

At age 13, his parents decided that he should attend Porter Military Academy in Charleston where discipline was an integral part of the educational process.

Charleston's *News and Courier* stated: "Archibald Rutledge, a graduate of Porter Military College, now a senior at Union College in Schenectady, N. Y., distinguished himself by recently taking first place in an oratorical debate. The topic: Advocating The Right of Secession.

At age 20, Rutledge graduated from Union College in June 1904. He immediately accepted a job as a substitute teacher for two weeks at Mercersburg Academy, situated in Pennsylvania's lower Cumberland

Valley. In the fall, Rutledge became head of the English Department, a position he retained for 33 years.

Rutledge married Florence Louise Hart in 1907, the same year he received his Master's Degree. In later years, he was the recipient of honorary degrees from sixteen universities and colleges. In 1930, he received the John Burroughs Medal, a national award for the best nature writing of the year.

In 1934, Governor I.C. Blackwood notified Rutledge that he had been appointed Poet Laureate of South Carolina -- an unusual event since he was still a resident of Pennsylvania.

During the annual family Christmas visit to Hampton in 1934 (unoccupied since 1930), his beloved wife became ill and died in Charleston.

Rutledge, whose nickname was Flintlock, married Alice Lucas in 1936. They were childhood sweethearts when he lived at Hampton, and she lived at a nearby plantation.

In the spring of 1937, Mercersburg Academy awarded him a pension. The S.C. Legislature granted him a stipend for services as Poet Laureate, a title he held for 39 years. With these two sources of income he was able, at long last, to return to Hampton, a place he always considered his spiritual home.

Upon their return, they discovered plaster had fallen from ceilings and walls. Weeds and small trees blocked the entrance. At age 53, Rutledge was well and strong. With the help of family and dedicated friends, they worked to restore Hampton to its original beauty.

After the death of his second wife in 1969, Rutledge conveyed the Big House and 275 acres to his beloved State of South Carolina in 1970. As a lover of nature and beauty, he felt Hampton belonged in the public domain.

Fifteen years earlier, the summer place in The Village had been sold. The week that Hampton became the property of the State, the summer place came on the market. With no real home, "Flintlock" purchased the property by telephone and thanked his Guardian Angel, of which he was a great believer.

At age 87 and in failing health, Rutledge returned to his birthplace in McClellanville on Jeremy Creek. He died September 15, 1973 at the summer place in The Village.

There is a special poem in *Veiled Eros* that I have enjoyed. It is listed below:

JASMINE AND PINE

In the home-woods at Hampton, I remember,
Out of a thicket of holly and of bay
Towered a lonely pine. He climbed the blue
Magnificently in his strength superb.
And to his might there clung with clambering grace
A delicate jasmine, frail and feminine.
She wrapped him tenderly, and thus arose
Until the two seemed one. His power sustained her,
While he with beauty was adorned. It seemed
To be his own, but really was of her.

Now many a year has gone. The giant pine
Again I see, the vine still banding him.
A storm has shown his crest. Forlorn he stands,
A ruined champion, pregnable and sad.

But now supporting, clinging close, upholding
His failing strength, the jasmine's beauty climbs,
As if to shield from foes his impotence.
For often proudest power is sustained
By frailest love, and crashes gloomily
If ever once that tender comfort fail.

Whenever I see the jasmine and the pine,
They make me think of husband and of wife.

I Remember Myrtle Beach When ...

Harness Horse Racing

In the mid-1930s, Paul and Parrot Hardy of Mullins, S. C., leased land from Myrtle Beach Farms Company between 21st and 27th Avenues in Myrtle Beach. On that site, they constructed the Washington Park Horse Race Track. They spent approximately $40,000 to make the park a first-class facility.

In the spring of 1938, the Myrtle Beach Racing Association invited sportsmen and lovers of harness racing from six states to inspect the completed project. Representatives from the Carolinas, Virginia, Pennsylvania, Ohio and Maryland attended the get-together.

In harness racing, horses pull small two-wheeled vehicles called sulkies. There are two styles, or gaits, of harness racing called trotting and pacing. The skillful driver is one who can train his horse to trot or pace to its limit of speed without breaking into a gallop.

The delegates assisted the association in formulating racing plans for the new facility. They had high praise for the track and proclaimed it as one of the best they had ever seen.

At that time, Myrtle Beach was the largest unincorporated town in the United States. The town was having growing pains, but many people did not want to incorporate. The first attempt failed. After much fanfare, the second attempt proved successful in 1938.

During the summer, the races began promptly at 2:30 p.m. on Wednesdays and Saturdays. *The Myrtle Beach News*, a weekly paper, publicized racing information.

A festive crowd of 5,200 excited fans paid a dollar admission and filled the overflowing steel grandstand for the opening day of Washington Park Race Track on June 3, 1938. The track's slogan,

DR. J. MARCUS SMITH

"Where The Turf Meets The Surf" appeared on the program.

The design of the stand allowed an unobstructed view of the races from the starting line to the home-stretch and the Atlantic Ocean, which it faced. A white vertical board fence surrounded the park. Early arrivals parked their cars diagonally against the fence. The overflow crowd for the Wednesday and Saturday afternoon races parked across the gray-sand Oak Street, then known as Little River Road. They maneuvered their cars among the pines and scrub oaks on the site of today's Convention Center.

The entrance to the grounds faced west. The actual track began near 21st Avenue and Oak Street. A white wooden rail outlined the one-half mile oval track. The far end curved near the side entrance of the former Myrtle Square Mall. The business office and 150 stables, which housed more than 100 horses, extended north to 27th Avenue.

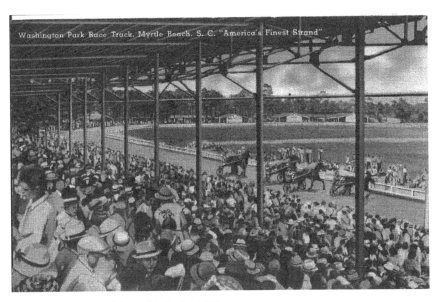

Postcard courtesy of Susan Hoffer McMillan

Along with my parents and friends, we attended the grand opening of the Washington Park Race Track. I sat on the top row in the stands. A cooling and refreshing sea breeze tamed the hot sun. The roof covered two-thirds of the back section of the grandstand.

Beyond the small pines trees on the far side of the track, I had an unobstructed view of the Atlantic Ocean. The rows of cottages and guesthouse were visible of either side of Ocean Boulevard.

A 15-foot sandy passageway extended between the box seats in the grandstand and the rail. The walkway led to a large sandy area, which housed a concession stand, pari-mutuel betting windows and a large odds board.

The names of the entries were posted on the board. A track official ascended the steps to a scaffold. With chalk, he entered the current odds on the horses.

Midway along the grandstand and directly across the track at the finish line stood the judges stand, which resembled a large gazebo on 6-foot pilings. The official announcer, C. A. Hopkins, operated the PA system. Also, the official photographer stood ready for a photo finish

Prior to the race, the names of the horses and drivers were announced over the public address system, as they paraded in front of the grandstand. C. McLaurin, the official starter, would strike the heavy iron bell to signal the beginning of the event.

Over the public address system came recorded music---"Washington Post March" and "Stars and Stripes Forever." Governor Olin D Johnson, along with Burnet R. Maybank, Mayor of Charleston and Myrtle Beach's Mayor Dr. W. L. Harrelson attended the grand opening. Carolina's young ladies, official pages, paraded the entries on the track.

Keyed up fans in the betting area often observed the horses and studied the odds on the board. Lines formed at the eight pari-mutuel windows. Spirits were high before the opening race.

On opening day, three races of three heats each were run, for a total of nine races. In the first race, Symbol Earl, owned by C. McLaurin of Minturn, S.C., won all three heats, easily outdistancing the other six horses. The purse for the owner was $250. Other favorites were Volo Hedgewood, Frisco Henley and Johnnie C. Frisco.

The success of the 1938 season proved to be greater than expected. The attendance and popularity of the track increased the following two years. More horses arrived from up and down the East Coast. The 1940 season opened on May 18th.

The Hardy brothers invited farmers and patrons of the track to be their guests on the third annual "Tobacco Growers Day" on June 12th.

The 1941 season opened with a cloud hanging over the park. Headlines in the Conway *Horry Herald* stated: "Sheriff enjoined from arresting." A proposed measure to legalize pari-mutuel betting in Myrtle Beach and throughout the state failed to become law. A temporary injunction kept the sheriff's department from interfering with the usual operation of the Myrtle Beach Race track. Racing continued through the 1941 season before the track officially closed. It was the end of harness racing in Myrtle Beach.

Let's Go Crabbing

Indians and early settlers discovered the abundance of crabs, fish and oysters in Horry County's coastal waters. Wildlife was plentiful, and it provided many people with a livelihood as well as recreation.

P.G. Winstead, a Myrtle Beach businessman and city councilman in the early '40s, told me a story about crabbing at Singleton Swash.

In the late '40s, "Plez," and his wife Jean and young daughter traveled the Kings Highway and turned towards the ocean on Lake Arrowhead Road. The sandy, rutted trail rambled around massive sand dunes and ended near the northern bank of Singleton Swash.

Winstead said, "The water was teeming with large shellfish. Our bushel basket was quickly filled."

At her parents' request, Martha removed her jeans. They tied the legs, so they could put the surplus crabs in them.

The episode made me recall my pre-teen years at the swash in the late '30s.

My parents loaded several crab nets and a bushel basket in the old four-door black Ford. Leaving Conway, we headed for Myrtle Beach on the long winding road.

Approaching Socastee, we passed the Methodist church. A sandy road with deep ruts branched off to Murrells Inlet, where we often spent afternoons crabbing from the weather worn piers. We stayed on the paved road and passed the Socastee School and continued our trip to the beach for a fun-filled crabbing afternoon at Singleton Swash. The remaining nine miles seemed short.

On Kings Highway, the present southbound lane was the only paved road. It ended at the entrance to the Ocean Forest Hotel, which was demolished in 1974. As we circled the majestic castle-like structure, my father commented, "This is called the Million Dollar Hotel." My mother replied, "It costs five dollars for one night's lodging."

In front of the hotel, a rough sandy entrance led to the beach. We had checked the tide table. It was one hour before low tide.

We had a beautiful drive as we headed north on the strand. Nature dominated the beachfront. The cooling salty sea breeze provided air-conditioning.

The roar of the motor frightened hundreds of sea gulls, but they found refuge above the breakers until we passed.

Two miles later, we drove across the shallow watery mouth of Singleton Swash, which George Washington crossed in 1791 on his Southern tour.

Climbing the huge sand dunes was like ascending small mountains. Cumulus white clouds drifted lazily in a blue summer sky. Once at the top, amid sea grass and sea oats, we looked down on the flowing blue-gray water. Sea gulls circled the marsh area. Egrets and herons waded in the shallow water searching for fish.

The inlet extended slightly south, and the longer northern end curved and moved inland. Green marsh grass fringed the back borders.

We could see that ebb tide was near. The crabs moved swiftly in the shallow water, which flowed to the mouth of the swash. With three nets in action, it did not take long to scoop up a basketful of large blue-shelled crabs, as they moved out with the tide.

We put the live crabs and gear in the trunk of the car. We left at low tide driving through the shallow water again.

As I looked through the rear view window, I saw Singleton Swash gradually fade from view. Before me, the Ocean Forest Hotel appeared taller and taller, as we approached the exit from the beach.

The humming of the motor, the swishing of the tires and the refreshing salt air always made me sleepy. As we traveled home, the crabs stirred and scratched in the basket. The sounds awakened me to thoughts of "good eating" and future crabbing trips.

VI.   The War Years   (1940s)

Marcus and Frankie Smith (1940s)

Mom and Dad graduated from Conway High School in 1942. They were both 16 years old at the time. Mom went off to Coker College in Hartsville, SC, where she attended for two years. She was always very homesick. Dad went off to the University of South Carolina and studied for a year before he took the train to Memphis in 1943 to attend the Southern College of Optometry. The college was a one building campus. Dad studied and  graduated from there in 1946 with an O.D. degree. He loved his time in Memphis. To make money to pay for his tuition, Dad he worked as an usher at a movie theatre.

 After graduation, Dad returned to South Carolina with the intention of opening his Optometry practice. He took the professional exam and was certified by the S.C. Board, but they subsequently found out that he was only 20 years old – not legally able to practice his profession. So he worked with Dr. Elmgren in

Columbia until he turned 21. Then he moved to Myrtle Beach and opened up his practice in the Arcade Building in 1947.

Gurley and Maude Johnson with Aubrey, Mom, Mary (Bebe) and Jack (late 1940s)

DR. J. MARCUS SMITH

Conway Theaters

Many years ago, the theater marquee in a small town was a focal point in the community. Movie houses served as a recreational center. Local folks gathered for movies, stage shows, concerts, and meetings.

In the latter part of 1914, H. G. Cushman moved to Conway and built the Pastime Theater. Corrugated galvanized roofing covered the sides of the building and the roof. The small entrance faced Main Street.

The year 1916 provided much entertainment for residents of Conway. According to the report in the *Horry Herald* in 1916, the Casino Theater, owned by McQueen Quattlebaum, offered the Billie Burke's series picture, *Gloria's Romance,* Gold Rooster plays and the great series picture, *Who's Guilty?* The Horry County Live Stock Improvement Association met in the theater in May. On October 16, the *Horry Herald* reported the first Lyceum Course for the season, at the new Pastime Theater, would be the Lowry-Lawrence Entertainers. Prior to the Christmas season, a company of vaudeville players performed two nights at the theater.

In 1926, the theater offered Charlie Chaplin movies. A Conway band supplied the music. Admission charge: 10 and 20 cents. In December 1926, an article in the *Horry Herald* stated: "Two brand-new and greatly improved moving picture machines were installed at the Pastime Theater last week. They run noiselessly. There are no stops for mending broken film."

The Shirley Temple movies in the mid-30s drew large crowds. Everyone liked *The Little Colonel* and *Bright Eyes,* during which she sang *On the Good Ship Lollipop.*

Younger children believed the theater's name was appropriate because it was always past time starting.

As the years passed, the theater became outdated. Cushman opened the Carolina Theater across the street (408 Main St.) on Aug. 6, 1936. *Private Number*, starring Robert Taylor and Loretta Young, delighted the packed house on opening night. A Jane Withers movie, *Little Miss Nobody*, was playing at the Pastime Theater, which closed as the end of the week.

Years later, Bish Anderson and the Holliday Brothers of Galivants Ferry bought the Carolina Theater from Cushman. The City of Conway continued to grow. John Monroe and Joseph Holliday built a new theater in 1947. The Holliday Theater, located at 335 Main Street, opened in October with the movie, *The Foxes of Harrow*, starring Maureen O'Hara and Rex Harrison. The new theater contained a soundproof room for people with crying children.

The Holliday Brothers operated both theaters for a while. Later, they closed the older Carolina Theater in 1965.

Eventually multi-screen theaters ousted the old matinee-style downtown cinemas. The movie industry stopped delivering movies to single screen theaters. The Holliday Theater closed on Labor Day 1986.

DR. J. MARCUS SMITH

A Spy on the Beach

Sunday school, Church services, a mid-day family meal and a leisurely afternoon was a typical Sunday for Horry County residents.

On a particular Sunday, December 7, 1941, the astounding news of the Japanese attack on Pearl Harbor shocked the nation.

Congress acted swiftly and declared war on Japan and the other Axis powers, Germany and Italy. Congress had passed the Selective Service Act in 1940, so troops were mobilized quickly.

South Carolina had registered more than half a million men, of whom 137,638 were inducted into service between 1940 and 1946. Brig. Gen. Holmes B. Springs of Myrtle Beach served as administrator for South Carolina.

While Germany controlled most of Europe and North Africa, Japan rampaged across Asia and the Pacific. The newly formed S. C. Defense Force enforced the new regulations in Myrtle Beach. Oceanfront residents were required to lower black window shades at night. National Defense mandated that motorists darken the upper half of car lights. When sirens sounded along the boulevard during the night, residents were alerted to turn off all lights.

German U-boats attacked U.S. shipping despite a vigilant Coast Guard. In the early part of 1942, almost 60 Allied ships and two U-boats were sunk off the North Carolina coast.

There were persistent reports that submarines came close to shore. An observation tower was located on the third floor of the Sea Side Inn. Volunteers used binoculars to scan the ocean searching for German submarines.

Suspicious drifters lurking near the beach were carefully watched. Residents viewed the few German immigrants with distrust. The German prisoner of war camp established in Myrtle Beach underscored the reality of war.

Rumors spread rapidly along the coast and sometimes became accepted as fact. A headline in the *Horry Herald* stated, "Rumors float about refueling of Axis." The article said: "Rumors have been floating around in regard to the arrest of certain persons near the Horry-Georgetown County line charged with having furnished gasoline and other supplies to Axis submarines operating in the Atlantic Ocean."

Rumors of German submarines off the coast troubled everyone. Residents sometimes observed the sudden flare of an explosion on the horizon. Later, they watched for the telltale oil or bits of wreckage on the strand. The *Horry Herald* reported that an unidentified body had washed up north of Myrtle Beach and was guarded by two soldiers.

Over and over again, people asked: "Could the Nazis be receiving help from someone locally?"

After Pearl Harbor Day, I often thought of an incident that occurred during the summer of 1941. My parents operated a second row guesthouse, *The Geneva Cottage*, on North Ocean Boulevard.

My living quarters consisted of a small room in the back of the house that faced the large sand dunes on the third row. I often fell asleep listening to the melodious sounds of music that drifted from a nightclub across the single paved lane on Kings Highway.

Behind the cottage, our garage had been converted into small apartments. Two ladies from North Carolina operated a boarding house across the Boulevard. My parents rented the small efficiency to their summer employees.

Often I watched a short stocky woman enter her room after her evening duties. As a 15 year-old, I thought, "That little old woman with such big feet is the ugliest thing that I have ever seen."

During most of the summer, she occupied the room. The guesthouse operators became suspicious of the unusual activities. Their employee quickly disappeared.

According to my parents and neighbor gossip, the lady in question proved to be a man. Evidence found in the room indicated that "he" was a German spy.

Rumors continued to float along the Grand Strand. Many of them were without foundation. The incident of the German spy still lingers in my mind

Myrtle Beach's First Airport

In July of 1996, the late Dr. Wilford LeRoy Harrelson was memorialized during a ceremony at the Myrtle Beach International Airport. Col. W. LeRoy Harrelson, son of Dr. Harrelson, along with 19 family members, friends and local citizens witnessed the unveiling of his portrait, which will occupy a prominent spot on the wall of the passenger terminal.

The Myrtle Beach Mayor, the late Bob Grissom, welcomed the group. Pete Winters, then Airport Director, addressed the gathering of 100 people. Winters announced that the connector road between Highway 17 By-Pass and the Myrtle Beach International Airport would be named W. LeRoy Harrelson Boulevard.

After Myrtle Beach became a municipality on March 12, 1938, Dr. Harrelson served as the first mayor. The six councilmen were B. B. Benfield, R. H. Cannon, R. M. Hussey, Jr., Dr. W. A. Rourk, J. C. Macklen and A. P. Shirley. During his two terms of office, Harrelson and council members acquired substantial land to construct a local airport.

After the completion of the project, a stone marker identifying the new facility as Harrelson Municipal Airport was placed at the original entrance on U. S. 17.

In the uneasy days of the 1940s, the international situation worsened. The government sought land for military bases. Myrtle Beach officials offered the airport for use in this time of national need. The property was transferred and the name altered for federal use. The original stone marker was removed.

DR. J. MARCUS SMITH

On November 3, 1943, thousands of acres of land officially became Myrtle Beach Army Airfield. It provided a training base for fighter planes and a bomb and gunnery range operated by the Army Air Corps.

Harrelson, a pharmacist, and his family moved to Myrtle Beach in 1927 from Marion, SC, where he had operated Harrelson's Drug Company. Other early pioneers who moved to the resort town in 1927 were Brig. Gen. Holmes B. Springs, a real estate developer, Dr. W.A. "Bill" Rourk, and Col. T.M. "Max" Jordan.

Harrelson, along with former Gov. Ransome J. Williams, opened the first pharmacy in Myrtle Beach -- Delta Drug Store -- on Broadway, now Main Street. Several years later, Harrelson opened another pharmacy – Colonial Drug Company – near the former location of the H.B. Springs Company building on Kings Highway.

Harrelson's daughter, the late Mary Elizabeth Hinson, and Roy Jr. entertained many friends in their home. Harrelson and his wife "Hatsy" were gracious hosts. Teenagers always found a welcome mat out for them at the Harrelson's. I know, because I was one of them.

Harrelson was one of the pioneers who had a vibrant vision for the future of Myrtle Beach. He died in 1945 before he saw the total fruition of his labors.

As Col. Harrelson, a Citadel graduate, stood by his father's portrait at the dedication ceremony at the Myrtle Beach International Airport, he said, "The vision and enterprise of Myrtle Beach's first municipal leaders in founding this airport in 1938-1939 are coming to fruition before our very eyes as this nationally pace-setting artery for air travel and commerce spearheads our area's thrust into the future."

Even though Harrelson Municipal Airport no longer exists, the connector road between Highway 17 By-Pass and the Myrtle Beach

I Remember Myrtle Beach When ...

International Airport bears the name of former mayor W. LeRoy Harrelson.

DR. J. MARCUS SMITH

Mr. Joe White

Photo courtesy of *The Sun* News

The former 10th and 11th Avenues North were renamed Mr. Joe White Boulevard in memory of a longtime resident of Myrtle Beach.

With a snap of his cloth in 1992, Joe *White put the finishing touches on my* shoes – in Woody's Arcade Barber Shop. The charge was two dollars. Joe first shined my shoes in 1947 for ten cents. The price of a shoe shine had changed, but White's personality had not.

After heart by-pass surgery in 1994, White returned to his job. Eventually declining health required him to vacate his shoeshine station. Julius W. "Joe" White died on December 23, 1997, at the age of 87.

Joe and his wife, Louise, moved from Georgetown to Myrtle Beach in 1930. He pursued his trade as a cobbler and accepted a job with Dorman's Barber Shop, which was next door to Seven Seas Restaurant on Broadway (now Main Street). Joe moonlighted and served as a waiter at the then recently opened Ocean Forest Hotel.

Years later, Joe moved across the street and became associated with Huggins' Barber Shop, which was next door to Dr. Bill Rourk's office in the Chapin Building.

In 1947, Sherwood Forrest built the Forrest Building just north of the Methodist Church. At the time, many citizens thought that the complex was too far away from the business district to be successful. Stores fronted on Kings Highway and an arcade in the building provided office space. W. S. Lamb opened the Arcade Barber Shop, and Joe joined him after spending several years at R. D. Bone's Barber Shop on 9th Avenue.

Photo courtesy of Jack Thompson – All Rights Reserved

I met Joe when I opened my office in the Arcade of the Forrest Building in 1947. Our friendship continued for many years. We joked about working in the Arcade of Sherwood Forrest. We had time to talk and discuss happenings in our small community.

He shared many memories of his Myrtle Beach years with me. He told me that he and Louise spent many hours dancing at Charlie Fitzgerald's Club. Apart from his regular duties, he worked part-time as a cook at the Kit Kat Hotel and spent many hours cleaning office windows. In our conversations, he said, "I have never owned a car and have no desire to get a driving license. My bicycle is all the transportation I need."

However, Joe did tell me an interesting story about a driving experience. In the early 1950s, Barry Sturmer, who operated a Men's Store on 9th Avenue North, planned a buying trip to New York City. Sturmer asked Joe if he would like to travel with him and visit relatives in New York. Joe accepted the offer. Along the way, Sturmer asked Joe if he would drive. White explained that he had never driven. As they traveled U.S. 17 on the return trip home, they heard someone comment in Virginia, "That's the first time I've ever seen a black man with a white chauffeur."

White became a shoe stylist for the stars who appeared at the Circle Theater in the Ocean Forest Hotel during the summer seasons in the 1950's. Among the stars were Robert Preston, Sidney Blackner, Arthur Treacher and Robert Webber. Famous orchestras appeared at the open-air Marine Patio in the hotel complex. White was a shoe stylist for Guy Lombardo, Russ Morgan, Johnny Long and others.

I have memories of him riding his bicycle around town, honking his horn as he greeted locals and visitors with a friendly smile and a warm handshake. He and I shared a friendship for more than 50 years – one I'll always cherish.

Summer of 1942

In the summer of 1942, law required the upper half of car headlights to be darkened before driving on the Boulevard at night. Oceanfront occupants were required to install black shades on windows facing the ocean. The recently formed S. C. Defense Force (known today as the State Guard) enforced the new regulation in Myrtle Beach.

Dim lights appeared in the amusement area, and a wooden observation tower stood on the south side of the pavilion. Volunteers used high-powered binoculars to look for enemy aircraft and German submarines. Often a wailing siren in the middle of the night required the dimming of all lights.

With the attack on Pearl Harbor by the Japanese on December 7, 1941, America was officially in the war. After the United States declared war on Japan, Germany and Italy declared war on America, and World War II was underway.

In the summer of 1942, the long twenty-one mile winding road still separated Conway from Myrtle Beach. The drawbridge at Socastee often slowed the flow of traffic. The distance between the two municipalities became greater, as gasoline stations in the eastern United States closed from 7 p.m. until 7 a.m., and tires were rationed.

The government recommended driving 35 miles per-hour to prolong the life of the tires. Later rationing extended to sugar and coffee, and gas was reduced to three gallons a week for non-essential driving.

At the end of May, Conway and Myrtle Beach High Schools prepared for graduation ceremonies. Conway graduated 117, while Myrtle Beach presented diplomas to 32. Prior to 1930, Myrtle Beach students completed their elementary education at the Beach and attended high school in Conway. Many traveled by train.

The average age of the graduates was sixteen, as the high schools in the County only required the completion of eleven grades for graduation. Many of the young men waited for their number to be called in the draft lottery, while a few enlisted.

The summer of 1942 saw the temporary closing of the Washington Park Horse Race Track. At the request of the Office of Defense and Transportation, the county fair in Conway was cancelled, along with all State Fairs.

The Carolina Theater in Conway and the Broadway and Gloria Theaters in Myrtle Beach provided recreational activities. During the summer of '42, moviegoers saw Joan Bennett and Cary Grant in *Suspicion*. Ronald Reagan and Ann Sheridan stared in *Juke Girl*. *Casablanca* and *Snow White and the Seven Dwarfs* drew big crowds.

Glenn Miller and his orchestra appeared in the movie, *Sun Valley Serenade*. *Chattanooga Choo Choo* and *I Know Why* were two big hits from the film.

Teen-agers listened and danced to juke box music at the pavilion. Popular songs included, *Sleepy Lagoon*, *Tangerine*, *Serenade in Blue*, *Moonlight Serenade* and *Blues in the Night*.

According to a July 1942 issue of Conway's *Horry Herald*, Belk's advertised men's sport shirts and ladies house dresses for one dollar and children school dresses for seventy-nine cents. Grocery stores listed their specials. Round steak and pork chops were 35 cents per pound. Other items included Merita bread for 11 cents. A box of corn flakes was 10 cents.

Fifty years have passed since the summer of '42. Graduation ceremonies will still occur in the month of May. Conway, a 4-A school, will graduate 364 students, while Myrtle Beach, a 3-A school, will present diplomas to 240 graduates.

The Conway High School Class of 1942 plans to hold its 50th class reunion at the Holiday Inn-West on May 2nd. A total of 74 will be attending, including four faculty members.

DR. J. MARCUS SMITH

Arcade Lunch Room

After being a "shiner of shoes" in Myrtle Beach since the 1930s, the late Joe White ended his career at Woody's Arcade Barber Shop as a "shoe stylist." During his 24 years at that location, we found time to visit.

Our conversation often drifted to food establishments near 10th Avenue North in the late 1940s and early l950s.

At the intersection of King's Highway and Broadway Extension, John's Bar-B-Que occupied a small block building. Customers parked in a small sandy area fronting the drive-up eatery.

John Angelo and his faithful employee, Edna Bellamy, stood behind sliding screen windows. Patrons shouted or walked to the outside counter to place their orders, then waited in their cars.

As John prepared the food, a cigar often dangled from his mouth. Edna bagged the completed order and yelled out, "Come and get it." Her out-stretched hand required the money before she handed the food to the customer.

Martha Baker Thomas, former Chair of the Art Department at Coastal Carolina University, said, "We often drove from Conway to eat the sauce-laden hot dogs and spicy minced barbecue."

John and Felecia Gravis immigrated from Greece and Poland. They met in New York and married before heading south. John's brother, Tom, and his partner had already established the Broadway Restaurant in downtown Myrtle Beach.

In 1947, The Gravises opened the Arcade Lunch Room in the Forrest Building. The small diner contained 10 counter stools and two tables. Unlike John's Bar-B-Que, they opened at 5:00 a.m. and closed at midnight. The Gravises did not own a car. From their residence on 4th Ave. North, they traveled by taxi.

Locals flocked to the popular lunchroom for their early morning coffee. Fishermen also enjoyed the tasty ham-and-eggs breakfast, with grits, before heading for the waters. By the time most offices had opened, community happenings had been discussed by businessmen and city officials. The Gravises became "Mom and Pop" to the numerous patrons.

Joe White, an employee at the Arcade Barber Shop, greeted me every morning when I arrived at my office, which faced City Hall. Visiting with Joe and having coffee in the lunchroom marked the beginning of my day.

Felecia and John's daily menu board hung on the wall. They inserted white letters in the black felt background. My daily task was to check the spelling on the menu.

One morning, the special of the day read, "Corned Beef and Garbage," which I corrected to cabbage. Another day, the menu of vegetables listed "stink beans," which was changed to string beans.

In 1948, LeRoy Letts opened the Pink House in the Forrest Building, which offered superb dining in an elegant atmosphere.

In the early 1950s, Johnny Burroughs leased a lot from Myrtle Beach Farms on the southeast corner of 11th Avenue and King's Highway. Previously, Johnny Holcombe's used car lot occupied the land.

Burroughs established Mammy's Kitchen Drive-In. The small dining area had eight stools. Along with drive-in service, the kitchen provided meals for prisoners at the Myrtle Beach jail.

Later, Burroughs sold the business to Chris Drosas and Chris Moshoures. They remodeled and enlarged the building, and Mammy's Kitchen became a restaurant.

Dwight Lamb, a well-liked photographer, operated Skip's Studio, on the south end of the Forrest Building. The establishment housed a lunch counter and gift shop.

Across King's Highway, Walgreen's Drug Store served lunches. Wilma's Cafeteria occupied the adjoining building. Later, it became Thomas Cafeteria.

Letts built a two-story brick colonial style Williamsburg structure on North Kings Highway at 43rd Avenue. The Pink House moved to the new location in the early 1950s.

John and Felecia Gravis and John Angelo retired in the early 1960s.

Only Mammy's Kitchen still stands as a reminder of the early eating establishments in the vicinity of the Forrest Building.

Guest and Boarding Houses

In the 1940s, guest and boarding houses had emerged along the Ocean Boulevard and downtown district in Myrtle Beach. Visitors returned every summer to their favorite abode, which usually served three meals daily. Boarding houses were numerous and provided the needs of local residents and summer employees.

George Inabinet, longtime resident said, "I moved to Myrtle Beach in the mid-forties and rented a room from Mrs. R.C. Couch. She operated "The Couch" at 503 7th Avenue North, across from Chapin parking lot."

Inabinet continued, "Later, several of us moved to the Welcome Inn at 905 N. Ocean Boulevard, which was in the center of the amusement area." Mrs. M. A. "Ma" Gause ran the Inn, while her husband supplied the produce from their Conway farm. The weekly rate was $17, which included the room and three meals. Inabinet said, "I enjoyed talking and girl-watching from the front porch."

Hilda Gause Avery, of Myrtle Beach, said, "My parents bought the property in 1929 for $4,000 and sold it in 1957."

Vance and Sally Norwood operated the Thomas Manor and several annexes on 8th Avenue. The two-story frame building faced the present amusement park of the Myrtle Beach Pavilion, which opened in 1949.

During the winter of 1948, I joined the Norwood family, who provided a home atmosphere for many local residents. The large floor furnace adequately heated the downstairs. Rising hot air took the chill off the six upstairs bedrooms. Several of the rooms overlooked the ocean and pavilion.

After a delicious evening meal, prepared by Sally and her daughters Ann and "Tootsie", we often gathered in the large living room. Lady Erle Green, a neighbor, came over and played the piano for us. We sang around an open fire on cold winter nights. Our dates were always welcome to join the fellowship.

The new high school on Kings Highway (present site of K-Mart) opened in 1948, without cafeteria facilities. Many of the faculty members, including the late Mary Long, and salesmen ate their noon meal at Thomas Manor.

Ted Jones, Minister of the Myrtle Beach Methodist Church, often dropped by to visit and have coffee with us. Jones assisted me in transferring my membership from the Conway Methodist Church.

During the summer of 1949, Hal McIntyre and his orchestra, direct from New York's Paramount Theatre, made several appearances at the Pavilion. The Grand Ole Opry Unit, from Nashville, presented two shows, followed by square dances.

Monday night was vaudeville time at the Pavilion with George Akers serving as Master of Ceremonies. Stage entertainment offered a variety of talent: slapstick, song-and-dance routines, juggling performances, and animal acts. Many of us attended vaudeville night.

One night The Three Stooges, "Curly, Larry and Moe," had top billing. After the show, Keith Cribb and I played carpet golf in the pavilion amusement park. The three stooges played ahead of us. Their antics on the golf course were unforgettable.

Recently I visited with Sally Norwood. I asked her to comment on the boarding house years. She said, "We were crazy to take on such a responsibility, but we enjoyed every minute of it." After Mr. Norwood's death, she moved from the Thomas Manor in 1952. She and her son-in-law, Dick Skillman, operated Ocean View Motel in Garden City until she retired at the age of 86.

Sally, who will be 97 years young on June 9th, is still a member of the First United Methodist Church in Myrtle Beach but attends Garden City Chapel, a block from her home.

After Hurricane Hazel ravaged the coast in 1954, guest and boarding houses declined. New and modern facilities developed along the oceanfront.

DR. J. MARCUS SMITH

Highway 501

The opening of the high rise concrete bridge over the Waccamaw River in Conway in 1938 eliminated the train-road drawbridge. These bridges connected to the 21-mile curving road between Conway and Myrtle Beach, by way of Red Hill and Socastee, which served the needs of the locals and tourists for many years.

In the early 1940s (the war years), many boats traveled the north-south Intracoastal Waterway, which opened in 1936. The Socastee drawbridge turned slowly and often to allow yachts, small freighters and barges, loaded with pulp wood, to pass along the popular waterway. As a result, summer traffic to the beaches backed up on the highway.

After several challenging years of construction through low-lying areas, Highway 501 opened in the fall of 1948. The new road more or less paralleled the train tracks and reduced the traveling distance between the two towns to 14 miles.

The late John Darden, chairman of the Conway Chamber of Commerce Road Celebration Committee, and the Myrtle Beach Chamber of Commerce planned a gala event. The grand opening of the new Conway-Myrtle Beach Road (Highway 501) took place on Wednesday November 10, 1948.

Motorcades, headed by Mayors Dr. Carl L. Busbee of Conway and Harry W. Tallevast of Myrtle Beach, left their respective towns at 1:50 p.m. They met midway on the new highway. The dignitaries mounted the speakers' stand at 2:00 p.m., while business and civic leaders exchanged mutual pledges of cooperation and goodwill.

General H. B. Springs, of Myrtle Beach, served as Master of Ceremonies. Springs recognized the Conway High School Band, who played the national anthem. The Rev. C. D. Brearley, Pastor of Myrtle Beach Presbyterian Church and a former pastor of Conway's Kingston Presbyterian Church, gave the invocation.

Springs introduced Claude R. McMillan, Chief Highway Commissioner, who spoke to the sizeable gathering. Springs recognized Shep Thompson of Georgetown, district highway commissioner. After the two mayors addressed the crowd, Paul Quattlebaum, Horry County Senator from 1936-1944, spoke briefly. He expressed his thanks for the cooperation between the towns and the involvement of the state highway department in the completion of the much needed project.

Senator Frank A. Thompson and Senator-elect Ernest Richardson of Conway shared the platform with other dignitaries. Ladies of the Conway and Myrtle Beach Garden Clubs planted trees to commemorate the occasion.

Claude R. McMillan cut the ribbon at the conclusion of the ceremony and officially opened Highway 501 between Conway and Myrtle Beach.

In the summer of 1949, the present Myrtle Beach Pavilion opened. Visitors flocking to the Grand Strand appreciated the new unswerving road, which revealed the beauty of the forest on either side. Many locals still traveled Highway 544 to Socastee and beaches on the South Strand.

In the early 1960s, people rejoiced when the new high-rise concrete bridge over the waterway at Pine Island was completed. In the event of hurricanes, exit routes would not be blocked by a malfunctioning bridge. In 1956, the State Highway Department had acquired right of ways and started construction of bridges over Highway 701 and the southern part of the Waccamaw River in Conway. The completion of the Conway by-pass moved the traffic from Main Street and expedited the flow of traffic to the coast.

It is the same road that leads to the beaches today -- Highway 501 -- 48 years since its official dedication that still serves as the main artery for traffic between Conway and Myrtle Beach.

Horse Racing Returns

Long-time residents in the Palmetto State remember the "good ole days" of horse racing in South Carolina. Pari-mutuel betting laws were largely ignored between 1936 and 1947. During those glory days, horse racing flourished all over the state.

During the years 1938 to 1941 and 1945 to 1947, Washington Park Race Track, with harness and jockey horse racing, dominated the scene in the rapidly developing city of Myrtle Beach.

People often asked the question, "Did the races exist in 1942, 1943 and 1944?" Harness racing left the Myrtle Beach area at the end of the 1941 season, after President Roosevelt declared war on Japan. Owners and drivers relocated to other tracks. Thoroughbred racing continued in some locations in the state. A few races were scheduled in Myrtle Beach in 1943.

The summer of 1945 revealed a new look at Washington Park Race Track. Thoroughbred racing, with jockeys, replaced harness racing. Pari-mutuel betting had been outlawed in the state.

Myrtle Beach town council adopted a rather unusual or unique ordinance providing for the sale of tickets or "receipts." Some officials considered it a clever scheme.

Bold headlines in the *Horry Herald*, "HORSE GUESSING," caught the attention of local readers. The newspaper article stated: "Contributions to support horse and dog racing have replaced old fashioned betting at the Myrtle Beach tracks"

The article continued, "Third Circuit Court Judge, J. Frank Eatmon, has signed a temporary injunction tying the hands of the State, County and local authorities from interfering with what was known as the 'Equal Mutual Guessing Game.'"

Again, the Hardy Brothers provided a full staff for the racetrack. M. O. Parsons served as track operator and manager. The 1945 season opened a little later than usual.

Myrtle Beach's first radio station, WMRA-AM, did not emerge until 1948. *The Myrtle Beach News*, a weekly newspaper, proved to be the only form of advertising.

In 1945, a new style of marketing appeared along the coastal area. The track management employed "Snookie" Martin to help advertise the races. Martin mounted speakers on top of his green panel truck. He drove slowly up and down the boulevard on race days and even to nearby towns.

With a microphone in one hand and a record player by his side, he played beach music to attract the attention. Between records, his booming voice informed the people of the racing slate for the day. You might say that he was the first Myrtle Beach Disc Jockey, a traveling D. J., on wheels.

On the sandy road just north of the park's main entrance, a wide gate led to the business office and stables. Early on race days, the secretary always posted the entries and their jockeys on the bulletin board in front of her office.

Early arrivals in the walking area grounds often saw Mackie Prickett of St. Matthews, Barbee Parsons of Hemingway, and Neil Bates of Wateree strolling around the grounds. Even though they hadn't begun to shave, they started racing competitively as mere youngsters. People referred to them as the "wonder jockeys."

Even though other states were represented at the track, South Carolina provided the most entries. They were from the stables of McIver Prickett of St. Matthews, M. O. Parsons of Hemingway, Dave Summers of Cameron, R. M. Schuler of Holly Hill, and C. E. McGill of Kingstree.

Two of the perennial favorites, "Excitement" and "Miss Carolina," always electrified the fans. Also there was "Cuantos," "Rookies Buddy," "Tango," "Corley's Pet," "Likely Lad" and "M. Longine."

The thundering hoofs of the thoroughbred "Excitement" often finished far ahead of the field. "Excitement" was a frequent winner at Belmont and Tropical Park.

Many fans attended the track on Farmer's Day in 1946. O. C. Calloway, Mayor of Myrtle Beach, welcomed the standing only crowd. As the featured speaker, Governor Ransome J. Williams addressed the people. He said, "Myrtle Beach is considered the fastest growing resort between Atlantic City and Miami. We need to have lots of entertainment and recreation, including horse racing."

In a 1980 article in *The Sun News*, the paper quoted remarks made by H. T. "Trez" Willcox, a long time Myrtle Beach resident and veteran newspaperman. He said, "How well do I remember Governor Williams' ringing words! Hundreds in the vast audience stood, clapped their hands and shouted in approval."

Fans eagerly awaited the grand opening of the 1947 season. Enthusiastic supporters filled the stands. They considered Washington Park Race Track as the best in the state. Even though it was off to a great start, it would be a photo-finish regarding the subterfuge of betting.

Earlier in the summer, Circuit Judge Frank Eatmon had handed down a favorable ruling allowing the races and betting to continue.

However, the court filed an injunction against the track on July 29, 1947. Then, the town of Myrtle Beach filed a subsequent petition. It stated: "Racing has existed for many years. State and anti-gambling laws have been around a long time. The town is at a loss to understand why some state officials are so anxious and determined to deprive the resort town of one of its best attractions for the thousands of visitors."

In August 1947, G. Dewey Oxner, Associate State Supreme Court Justice, handed down his decision banning betting on horse and dog races under whatever guise conducted. The new ruling marked the end of illegal betting. The dog track was located between 13th and 17th Avenues on South Kings Highway.

With the closing of the tracks, 125 employees and a weekly payroll of $7,000 vanished from the resort's economy. The horses were transported back to their home stables and other tracks.

After horse racing came to an end, tourists checked out of the boarding houses and the few hotels that operated at the time. For a while, it seemed like a ghost town.

The last partial visible landmark of the Washington Park Race Track was a view of pine trees curved around the southern end of the track. The Wachovia Bank now occupies that site. The steel grandstand was moved to the Myrtle Beach Speedway on U. S. 501.

The young jockeys also moved in different directions. After high school, Neil Bates attended the Naval Academy. He served 20 years in the military before retiring.

Barbee Parsons, a Methodist Minister, serves the S. C. Conference. Parsons told me that he still loves racing, but not the gambling.

I Remember Myrtle Beach When ...

Mackie Prickett retired from the racing circuit at the age of 13. Prickett was modest about his winning records as a young jockey, but his wife Jackie recently told me that he rode five winners in one afternoon.

Besides being an outstanding high school quarterback, Mackie Prickett was a star quarterback at The University of South Carolina in 1955 and 1956. He graduated with honors at the University, with a degree in Pharmacology.

It's a comfortable feeling in the year 2001, combining the past with the present, to park on the southern end of Myrtle Square Mall where fine horses once raced. You can almost hear the wheels turning on the sulkie carts. Upon entering the mall, you hear the footsteps of hurried shoppers trotting and pacing throughout. In the amusement court, you see the colorful carousel with the many beautiful horses, each with a rider going around and around.

VII. The Innocent Years   (1950s)

Marcus and Frankie Smith (1950s)

Mom and Dad were married on October 7, 1950 in the Conway Methodist Church. They first lived in the Patterson Apartments and then after a couple of years they moved into the Ross Haven, both in Myrtle Beach. They moved into their first house at 205-38th Avenue North (now the house number is 407) on September 23, 1954 – just a month before hurricane Hazel and almost two months before I was born.

The 1950s were a fun time for newlyweds and young marrieds in the small town of Myrtle Beach. Mom and Dad had a great group of friends who were always doing something together. Dad was a member of the Junior Chamber of Commerce (Jaycees), as were all his buddies. They were responsible for coordinating the Miss SC/Miss America pageant. The pageant was held at the Ocean Forest Hotel.

Mom and Dad were members of the First United Methodist Church of Myrtle Beach. They raised the three of us in this church, of which we are all still members. Dad was a Sunday School teacher for the youth and the counselor for the Methodist Youth Fellowship (MYF) for many years. He loved teaching and guiding the high school kids. They kept him young and active. He and Mom would have all the kids over for parties at our house, and the three of us boys got to see all the crazy teenagers cutting up.

He always prepared diligently for his Sunday School and MYF lessons, but he made sure the kids had fun too. He would have the teenagers sing Christmas carols in the middle of the summer, with the windows open in the classroom on the second floor of the Asbury building. He always treasured the memories and the friendships  *of these young adults. Many of these young adults have known the three of us for our entire lives, and we often heard how much Mom and Dad meant to them. You see, Mom was always the straight man for all of Dad's practical jokes. Dad got the laughs, but Mom always enjoyed the entire process.*

Dad and Jaycees at annual convention at the Ocean Forest Hotel
(Photo courtesy of Jack Thompson - All Rights Reserved)

DR. J. MARCUS SMITH

Carolina Circle Theater

On June 20, 1953, the hilarious Broadway hit *Bell, Book and Candle*, starring Robert Preston, opened the premier season of the Carolina Circle Theater.

Jane Barry Haynes, now a Grand Strand resident, came to Myrtle Beach in 1953 and formed the Myrtle Beach playhouse. The air-conditioned Ballroom of the Ocean Forest Hotel housed the most elegant theater in the southeast, which presented its plays in the round, or arena type seating.

From 1953 through 1959, ten plays were presented during the summer season. One cast rehearsed during the day, while the other performed at night.

Haynes said, "Most of the time, we got the original Broadway players. Top money for a show then was $3,000. Community involvement proved to be the key to the success of the theater. Myrtle Beach loved the playhouse and everyone responded."

The Myrtle Beach Jaycees actively supported the theater. Many of us had reservations for the Thursday night opening performance. Patrons paid $4.50 for the reserved section, while other seats were available for $1.50. We had the opportunity to visit with the stars following the play.

Jim Winslow, Robert Webber and other members of the resident cast assisted us in the Jaycee-sponsored Miss S. C. Pageant. Among other awards, the winner of the Pageant received a summer scholarship with the Circle Theater.

Mickey Spillane, who had moved to the Grand Strand during the 1950s, became an active supporter of the playhouse. The Theater did an original Mickey Spillane play entitled "The Bank at Silver Springs" in 1958.

Over the seven years, some of the stars that performed were Gloria Swanson, Sylvia Sidney, Miriam Hopkins, Arthur Treacher, Zasu Pitts, Shelley Winters and Veronica Lake. Sidney Blackmer made several appearances, along with Charlie Ruggles, the Gabors, Brian Donlevy, Frank Sinatra, Jr. and Barbara Britton. Jane Barry Haynes acted in many of the productions.

Well-known Broadway shows filled the stage. To mention a few: *Witness for the Prosecution, Teahouse of the August Moon, Miss Private Eye, A Streetcar Named Desire, and Blithe Spirit.*

Barbara Britton appeared in *Born Yesterday*, as the scatter-brained girlfriend of a mobster. After the show, the audience attended a breakfast in the spacious dining room of the Ocean Forest Hotel. The delightful Barbara Britton, who was dressed in a yellow sun back dress, visited each table chatting with the guests.

After she returned to New York, she mailed a hand-written letter to me, since I was Jaycee President. The letter was dated July 7, 1954.

> Dear Dr. Marcus,
>
> Now that I have finished my engagement at the Myrtle Beach Playhouse and have come on to New York, I want to again thank you and your Jaycee group for the part you had in making my stay at Myrtle Beach such a very pleasant one.
>
> It was so nice of you to meet me when I arrived and to send me the lovely flowers on my opening night. I shall indeed look forward to my next visit to Myrtle Beach.

DR. J. MARCUS SMITH

>Sincerely,
>Barbara Britton

The Ocean Forest Hotel needed the Ballroom for an expanded convention schedule in 1957, so the Playhouse moved to the Shrine Club for two years. In 1959, Haynes gave the playhouse to Myrtle Beach officials, but the rising cost of productions kept it from continuing.

Under the guidance of Jane Barry Haynes, the Playhouse was ranked nationally by Actors Equity, as seventh best in the star system for summer stock theaters.

The friendliness of the stars, the resident cast, and the participation of local support groups provided seven years of outstanding entertainment for the Grand Strand.

I Remember Myrtle Beach When ...

The Miss South Carolina Pageant

In the late 1940s, the SC Theater Exchange directed the Miss South Carolina Pageant between movies at the Palmetto Theater in Columbia. The Myrtle Beach Jaycees became interested in staging the Pageant in Myrtle Beach.

In September 1948, the late Eddie Benton, "Dub" Simpson, W. J. (Bill) Sigmon, Sr. and I attended the Jaycee State Board Meeting in Columbia. The Executive Committee met with Lenora Slaughter, then Director of the Miss America Pageant. We obtained the franchise for the S.C. Jaycees, and they awarded the sponsorship to the Myrtle Beach Jaycees. The first Jaycee-sponsored Miss S. C. Pageant took place in the Myrtle Beach Pavilion on August 11, 1950, with only five contestants competing for the title. Over 2,000 people crowded the auditorium and witnessed the crowning of Carolyn Fowler of Spartanburg as Miss S.C. 1950.

Fowler represented S.C. in the Miss America Pageant. That particular year, the Pageant officials decided to post-date the national pageant title. Yolande Betbeze (Miss Alabama) was named Miss America 1951.

Seventeen contestants entered the 1951 Pageant. Joyce Perry of Conway took first place honors. Perry finished among the top ten in Atlantic City.

The Pageant became a part of the Sun Fun Festival in 1952, and twenty-seven girls took part in the gala parade. Mary Kemp Griffin, of Florence, smiled and sang her way to the 1952 Miss S.C. Crown. Griffin made it to the top ten in the Miss America Pageant.

Local Jaycees and Jaycee-ettes spent endless hours, without pay, preparing for the Pageant. Local hotels donated free housing, and many provided luncheons and dinners for the contestants, judges, and guests.

Many local personalities performed between the preliminary judging on the three nights of competition. Harold Lewis, quarterback at USC, sang his way into the hearts of the large crowd.

In 1953, Miriam Stevenson from Winnsboro represented Greenwood and won the title. Stevenson was among the ten finalists in Atlantic City.

The following year, Miriam Stevenson entered and won the Miss S.C.-USA Contest. She went on to become Miss USA and represented the United States in the Miss Universe Pageant. The blue-eyed blonde was crowned Miss Universe.

Each year, the popularity of the Pageant continued to grow. Other Jaycee chapters were taking notice of the success of the Miss S.C. Pageant and became interested in securing the franchise for their city. We staged vigorous campaigns at the yearly Jaycee State Board Meeting in Columbia to retain the sponsorship.

The Pageant had grown to over thirty contestants in 1954. Rankin Suber, representing Columbia, walked away with the title and finished as 2nd runner-up to Miss America in Atlantic City.

The year 1955 proved to be another great year for the Pageant. Another Conway girl, Martha Dean Chestnut, represented S.C. in the Miss America Pageant and finished in the top ten. Marian McKnight, roommate of Martha Dean Chestnut at Coker College, represented Manning in the 1956 Pageant in Myrtle Beach. The curvaceous blonde did an imitation of Marilyn Monroe. The crowd roared its approval along with the judges. The same talent jolted the captive audience in the

Miss America Pageant. Marian McKnight was crowned Miss America 1957.

As Miss America, she returned to the Myrtle Beach Pavilion in June and placed the 1957 Miss S. C. crown on the head of Columbia's Cecelia Ann Colvert.

After eight successful years in Myrtle Beach, the local Jaycees campaigned hard to retain sponsorship, but the Greenville Jaycees offered Textile Hall, TV coverage, and more adequate facilities. The State Jaycees awarded them the sponsorship. Eventually, a private corporation secured the franchise.

DR. J. MARCUS SMITH

End of Summer

Myrtle Beach's year-round population slowly increased from 200 in 1926 to 3,400 in 1950. While I was at the office, my wife Frankie managed an apartment complex in 1952.

The summer season opened the first of June. The gigantic display of fireworks in front of the pavilion on Labor Day night concluded another summer season in the coastal resort.

We were often asked the question, "What do the locals do in the off season?"

The small town atmosphere became evident as many tourists left town to attend the running of NASCAR'S Southern 500 at the Darlington International Raceway, which opened in 1950. Many operators of guesthouses and businesses closed for the season. Year-round stores returned to half-holidays on Wednesday afternoons.

Locals, along with a scattering of tourists, turned to surf fishing, while others preferred fishing from the many piers. Shell collectors walked the wide beaches. Myrtle Beach schools opened on Sept. 4th with an enrollment of 1,267 students.

Superintendent J. Harry Spann announced that Earl Huggins, after many successful years, had retired as the Seahawks football coach. L. J. "Dutch" Funderburk assumed the duties at the high school and faced Olympic of Columbia in his first game.

Myrtle Beach's second drive-in theater, The Flamingo, opened between 77th and 79th Avenues North on the present site of Northwood Shopping Center. Myrtle Beach Drive-In Theater was located at 13th Avenue South.

I Remember Myrtle Beach When ...

The Parent-Teachers Association staged its annual Halloween carnival at the pavilion on Oct. 31. The proceeds benefited the schools. The Jaycees held their Thanksgiving turkey shoot on the beach in front of Gay Dolphin Gift Shop.

Photo courtesy of Jack Thompson - All Rights Reserved

Sloppy Joes's, a popular off-season gathering place, was located at the corner of Ninth Avenue and North Ocean Boulevard, the present site of Ripley's Believe It Or Not. The management advertised breakfast 24 hours a day, with the best coffee in town.

Sloppy Joe's also had a bingo parlor, which offered its facilities to the Jaycees each fall. Myrtle Beach merchants donated gifts for the weekly event. Locals flocked to the Monday night games.

The Myrtle Beach Ministerial Association sponsored community Thanksgiving services. In 1952, Rev. Eugene J. West conducted the service at the Episcopal Church.

On December 12th, Santa Claus headlined the Civitan-sponsored Christmas parade with its many floats, decorated convertibles and area bands. The parade began at the intersection of Broadway and U.S. 501, proceeded through the business district, and ended at the pavilion.

Myrtle Beach's two cinemas, Broadway and Gloria, provided winter entertainment for the local population.

As the winter turned to spring, guesthouse operators and seasonal businesses prepared for another summer season.

DR. J. MARCUS SMITH

Coastal Carolina College

As a senior citizen, enrolling for a credit course at Coastal Carolina College turned into a unique experience. Registration day brought back memories of fifty years ago at USC's main campus in 1942. Recently at Coastal Carolina, computers speeded up the process. Courteous and helpful students and administrative staff members made it a pleasurable event.

In the 1950s, I took courses at Coastal Carolina College, which had started holding classes in the Conway High School Building. So, in 1954, the high school was the home of a local college. With a small enrollment, the outlook was not promising, but the seed had been planted. During that time, Edward M. (Dick) Singleton served as principal of Conway High School. He worked hard, along with other lay and professional people, to make his dream of a college in Horry County come true.

The Coastal Education Foundation and Horry County Commission on Higher Education approached the University of S. C. and offered the backing of local strength. USC declined the offer. The College of Charleston agreed to become the sponsor of the new College. George Gries, then President of the College of Charleston, undertook to provide the new college with faculty members. Conway High School again provided the space.

During that period, I had the opportunity to take a late afternoon course in American History taught by Dr. Joe Lesesne, who is now President of Wofford College. Even though I had my college degree, my thirst for knowledge continued. Dr. Glen Webb's class in Biology and Genetics proved to be an interesting course. One Saturday, he scheduled a field trip to study the flora and fauna on the site where Coastal Carolina College now stands. I vividly recall one class when he walked to the chalkboard and wrote the letters "DNA" on the board and circled them. He faced the class and said, "Remember those letters, you will hear more about them in the future."

The College of Charleston withdrew its support in 1958. The Foundation and the Commission established the Coastal Carolina Junior College.

In 1960, a second approach to USC proved to be successful, and an extension center developed in Conway. Horry County teachers could take the courses necessary to renew their certificates, or work toward a graduate degree, which was very helpful.

Edward M. Singleton, Chancellor Emeritus of Coastal Carolina College of the University of South Carolina, was the first director of the tiny education center. It has grown from 80 original students in 1962 to more than 4,000 in 1990.

Edward M. Singleton and I grew up in the same neighborhood in Conway. We shared the same dormitory at the University of South Carolina in the early 1940s. Along with many others, I consider him to be the Father of Coastal Carolina College. He presided over its birth, saw it through its most difficult times, and continues to nurture it caringly.

In the early 1960s at the present College, I took a Music Appreciation course, taught by the late Dr. J. H. T. Mize. During a summer session, I had the privilege of taking a Western Civilization course under Dr. Charles Joyner, a noted author, who holds Ph. D. degrees in both history and folklore.

DR. J. MARCUS SMITH

I have had the opportunity to take third Quarter courses recently at the College. Several classes on Creative Writing, taught by an inspiring instructor -- Susan Meyers -- proved to be worth-while. Catherine Lewis's "History of Horry County" draws students of all ages.

On Tuesday night at the College, it's time for the 6:30 to 9:30 class on THE POETICS AND PERFORMANCE OF COUNTRY MUSIC. Twenty students, including teenagers, young adults and senior citizens, make up the class. Dr. Paul Rice, a masterful professor who likes to be called "Doc," teaches the course. "Doc" shares with us a background of country music and techniques of song writing.

Coastal Carolina College stands tall as one of the greatest achievements in Horry County in this century. As in the past, the instructors are top of the line. Young and old benefit from the educational opportunities that it offers.

Hurricane Hazel

In October 1954, Indian summer prevailed along the Grand Strand. Many guest house operators had closed their establishments. After a successful season, the small town atmosphere of Myrtle Beach became evident.

Locals, along with a scattering of tourists, turned to surf fishing, while others preferred fishing from the many piers. Shell collectors walked the wide beaches. The high school football season was well underway, Mayor Ernest Williams and council members debated local matters, and civic clubs were making plans for the off-season.

Hurricane Hazel had just rolled over the mountainous Republic of Haiti with destructive force and then weakened over the sea. She came ashore in Florida, not much more than a tropical storm, crossed the state and entered the Gulf of Mexico.

The fickle storm hesitated, changed her mind and moved back across the Florida peninsula. After she entered the Atlantic Ocean again, news media announced that Hurricane Hazel had gained strength but was moving northward.

After watching the 11 o'clock news from Charleston, the latest hurricane advisory stated that the storm should skirt the South Carolina coast. Frankie and I retired for the night at our 38th Avenue residence.

At 3 a.m., the morning of October 15th, the constant knocking on our front door awakened us from a deep sleep. When I opened the door, Allan Ericson, a friend and neighbor, informed us that the hurricane had stalled briefly and had turned towards the coast. He advised us to leave immediately.

Ericson knew that we were expecting our first child in a few weeks. Ericson later said "The hurricane could easily bring on early labor, and the trip to Conway could be catastrophic if the draw bridges over the Intracoastal Waterway on Highway 501 and Socastee malfunctioned."

Our bags were already packed, anticipating the blessed event. We loaded the car and headed for my parents' home in Conway. The trees were already yielding to the strong winds and heavy rain made traveling difficult. As we traveled down Kings Highway, City and County patrol officers passed us, with sirens screaming, alerting people of impending danger. Traffic did not present a problem, but the shadowy ride approaching Conway proved to be laborious. Prior to construction of the 501 By-Pass, the two-lane road, with water-filled gorges on either side, was frightening. The wipers were not effective against the gale winds, which rocked the car and blasted the windshield with torrential rain. With the side window down, I had to drive with occasional glances at the center white line on the highway.

We were relieved when we crossed the high-rise bridge in Conway and traveled down Main Street. We relaxed, because the hospital was only five blocks from the house (the Ocean View Memorial Hospital in Myrtle Beach did not open until 1958). We huddled around the portable radio searching for news. Myrtle Beach's WMYB lost its power at midnight. Conway's WLAT was off the air, so we tuned in Charleston stations. The latest report stated the fast moving hurricane would definitely cross the coastal area. It was now a category 4 storm.

Even as the sky turned gray, heralding the coming of day, the tops of tall pines began to toss as though reluctant to face the approaching storm. By 6:30 a.m., the 7th and last pier fell to the rambunctious hurricane.

I Remember Myrtle Beach When ...

Hurricane Hazel smashed into the Grand Strand on high tide at 10 a.m. Winds of 130 miles per hour drove heavy rains. Waves were estimated to have reached a height of 40 feet. Slabs of cement, once the sidewalk that ran the length of the Pavilion and the amusement park, were lifted like sheets of paper in the wind and hurled into beach-side stores.

We returned to Myrtle Beach at noon. We stood in line at the Police Department on 10th Avenue to secure a pass to return to our home.

Cars were still lined up at Chapin's Service station for gas. The electrically operated pumps were out at all other stations, and Charlie Singleton, with hand pumps, did a land-office business until power was restored.

On the oceanfront, many homes, cottages and guest houses were undermined. Dunes were leveled, with massive beach erosion. The oceanfront wooden boardwalk, which extended from 27th Ave. N. to 3rd Ave., floated out to sea.

Photo courtesy of Jack Thompson - All Rights Reserved

DR. J. MARCUS SMITH

A semblance of order now prevailed in Myrtle Beach. The storm's severity was not easily discernible except on the oceanfront. The beaches to the south and north of Myrtle Beach were hardest hit by the fickle Hazel. Eyewitnesses stated sand covered the roads and lots where front-row houses once stood. Second row houses were washed from their foundations and splintered by the waves.

Governor James F. Byrnes called out the National Guard, and guardsmen were positioned at strategic points along the beaches to prevent looting.

After the hurricane, a jokester posted a note on the City Hall bulletin board, which read: "Hazel caught Myrtle with her banks (Dunes) down." Another prankster added, "Witch Hazel."

Police Chief, W. C. Newton, told me, "If we didn't get the eye of Hurricane Hazel, we got the eyebrow."

The Grand Strand had survived the hurricane, and rebuilding began quickly, with many changes. Quaint wooden cottages and guest houses serving meals had disappeared. The "tourist homes" of the 1940s were replaced by high-rise modern hotels and beautifully landscaped motels.

It was a New Day and a New Era for the Grand Strand.

Myrtle Beach Meets Myrtle Beach

The year 1957 proved to be a banner year for queens at the annual Sun Fun Festival in Myrtle Beach. South Carolina's own Miss America, Marian McKnight, presided over the festival in which 41 queens from around the state vied for the Miss South Carolina crown.

"The Queen For A Day" TV program selected a queen on May 29th who would be an honored guest at the festival. The program, with host Jack Bailey, was televised five days a week from Hollywood over 142 stations and broadcast over 496 Mutual radio stations, coast to coast.

Mrs. Griffey Lewis of Shreveport, La. was selected the Sun Fun Queen For A Day. She arrived in Myrtle Beach on Piedmont Airlines in time for the parade and other festival activities.

In the spring of 1957, the Chamber of Commerce conducted a nationwide search for a person named "Myrtle Beach." A local panel of judges worked several months with the press, wire services, radio and TV networks.

A month prior to the festival, the committee announced the winner: Myrtle Beach, a blue-eyed brunette housewife from Fort Madison, Iowa. The committee furnished transportation for the winner and her family. Mr. and Mrs. LeRoy Letts, owners and operators of the Pink House at 4302 N. Kings Highway, provided lodging for the Iowa family.

Beach worked in a department store and faithfully served her Methodist Church and PTA. A committee member said "One of the primary reasons we selected this Myrtle Beach was because her family represents a typical American family."

Beach, wife of R.D. Beach, was chosen from 17 entries from 11 states. Five came from North Carolina and two from South Carolina.

The Beaches' teen-age girls -- Sandy, 17, Marshy, 13, and their son, Rocky, 10---accompanied their parents to the festival.

The May 29th edition of *The Myrtle Beach News* quoted the chosen Myrtle: "The first clue to your contest came from my cousin in Sioux Falls, S. D., and Dr. L.C. Niddert. His relative from Seneca read about the search in the paper and mailed it to me. I received numerous local calls and letters from people who had read the article in the *Chicago Tribune*."

The Chamber of Commerce received a letter from a friend and neighbor of Beach. She said, "Myrtle Beach is a very personable woman, a fine patient understanding mother of three nice youngsters. Our Myrtle has a marvelous personality. She radiates cheer and happiness at all times."

The late Isla and Larry Boulier escorted the Beach family on a tour of Brookgreen Gardens. Boulier, editor of *The Sun* Newspaper, wrote an article on the Beaches. He said, "Prior to their departure, Paul Manson of NBC's radio program 'Monitor' made a tape of the family's impression of Myrtle Beach." Boulier continued, "Mrs. Myrtle Beach and family are now on their way back to the rolling corn fields of Iowa, with their lives enriched by their experiences as guests of Myrtle Beach and its citizens."

After their brief reigns, the other "queens" left Myrtle Beach. Mrs. Griffey Lewis, "Sun Fun Queen For A Day," returned to Louisiana. Marian McKnight, Miss America, continued her scheduled tours throughout the United States before relinquishing her crown at the Miss America Pageant in September.

I Remember Myrtle Beach When ...

1957 Sun Fun Festival

The Chamber of Commerce, City of Myrtle Beach, Jaycees and other local organizations and businesses staged the sixth annual Sun Fun Festival June 5-9 in 1957. The program offered a wide variety of activities for all ages.

On Wednesday morning, the Dunes Golf and Beach Club hosted the Amateur Handicap Golf Tournament, while the Ladies Invitational Golf Tournament took place at the Pine Lakes Country Club. Contestants began to arrive for the Miss South Carolina Pageant.

In the afternoon, the Ocean Queen Cruise Boat, docked at Vereen's Marina, offered free trips for children. The new multi-million dollar Myrtle Beach Air Force Base opened its doors to the public. Ken "Sharecropper" Lovell's Band provided music for the evening street dance on 9th Avenue North.

City officials designated Thursday as Sun Fun Day and issued a proclamation requiring all inhabitants to wear beach attire, bathing suits or shorts between dawn and noon in down-town Myrtle Beach. Festival lady cops quickly arrested violators and escorted them to the Sun Fun Court, where they were tried and sentenced by Father Neptune.

Guilty culprits landed in The Sun Fun Jail, known as "Davy Jones' locker." Among the inmates were Mickey Spillane, beauty contestants and local dignitaries.

Mom and Dad at the Sun Fun Jail

Mermaids collected the one-dollar fine and placed the money in a sea chest for local charities. The festival "slammer" stood in front of the small frame Chamber of Commerce Building on the east side of Kings Highway, near 9th Avenue North.

The State Junior Chamber of Commerce held the franchise for the Miss South Carolina Pageant, which highlighted the Sun Fun Festival. The local Jaycees had been awarded the sponsorship since 1950. Myrtle Beach had become known as "Home Of The Miss South Carolina Pageant."

On Friday morning, thousands of fun-loving people witnessed the mile-long Sun Fun parade, with its dazzling floats and tuneful marching bands. On the premier float, Marian McKnight, Miss America 1957, stood and waved to the cheering crowd. The pageant committee had rolled out the royal red carpet for their Palmetto Queen. Forty-one contestant hopefuls vying for the Miss South Carolina crown rode in their special convertible, just as Marian McKnight had the previous year, when she represented the City of Manning.

On Thursday and Friday evenings, preliminary judging took place on the stage of the Myrtle Beach Pavilion. During their stay in the resort city, the contestants were surrounded by an aura of pageantry, celebrities, public appearances, luncheons and a seemingly endless succession of rehearsals.

Dancing under the stars at the Ocean Forest Hotel Marine Patio proved to be a popular feature of the festival on Thursday evening. The Masquerader's Ball, for members and guests, took place in the ball room of the Ocean Forest Hotel on Friday night.

I Remember Myrtle Beach When ...

The Human Checker Game at the Myrtle Beach Pavilion Terrace spotlighted the Sun Fun schedule on Saturday morning. The first twenty-four entries in the pageant served as pawns in the well-liked event.

Cecelia Ann Colvert, Miss Columbia, won the Miss South Carolina title amid thunderous applause from an estimated crowd of 3,000 at the pavilion in the Saturday night finals. Miss America, our own Marian McKnight, placed the crown on the head of the new Miss South Carolina. The contestants attended church services on Sunday morning, and then headed for their respective homes, as the sixth annual Sun Fun Festival came to a close.

After eight successful years in Myrtle Beach, the local Jaycees campaigned hard to retain sponsorship of the pageant, but the Greenville Jaycees offered Textile Hall, TV coverage and more adequate facilities. The state organization awarded them the 1958 franchise.

After many years, another private corporation secured the franchise. At the present time, they are looking for a new location for the pageant. Who knows, it could be returning to its former home.

DR. J. MARCUS SMITH

Return of the Braves

After more than 50 years, Braves baseball returns to Myrtle Beach. Coastal Federal Field will serve as home for the Pelicans, an Atlanta Braves Class A Farm team, with the first home game scheduled for April 12th, 1999.

The Braves first came to Myrtle Beach in the 1940s. In those uneasy days, the town's tiny municipal airport was made a part of the National Defense Program. On November 3, 1943, thousands of acres of land officially became Myrtle Beach Army Airfield. It provided a training base for fighter planes and a bomb and gunnery range operated by the Army Air Corps. After the end of World War II, the base officially closed in November 1947. The acreage reverted to the city of Myrtle Beach, and E.A. "Tony" Anthony served as manager of the property. Harry Jenkins, director of the Boston Braves Tribal Baseball System, negotiated with Anthony for use of some base land.

On December 23, 1949, *The Myrtle Beach News* reported, "An agreement for the return of the Boston Braves Farm Clubs to Myrtle Beach next spring (1950) has been executed." Jenkins said, "We look forward to returning and plan larger expenditures to make the Myrtle Beach layout one of the best in the country."

John W. Mullen, a young assistant in the minor league department, joined the Braves organization in 1947. Mullen played an important role in the development of the training facility.

Rugged frame structures in the hospital area of the abandoned Airfield housed the young athletes. The old lecture and movie hall served as a cafeteria the first year. Before the next season, Bill Driver headed the committee to install a $10,000 modern kitchen.

Later he said, "Feeding 200 ball players three meals daily for six weeks is a big job." A typical evening meal included soup, chef's salad, roast beef, baked potatoes, carrots, string beans, bread and apple pie.

At the end of the present runway (near Kings Highway), the Braves Club constructed four first-class baseball fields in the shape of a cross. A tall observation tower stood in the center of the complex.

Outfielders, infielders, pitchers and catchers wore different colored caps. John Quinn, general manager of the parent club, and other officials viewed the athletes in action and determined their farm league assignments.

The Braves invited the public to visit the training grounds. Local officials placed a quarter-page ad in the local paper that stated, "Welcome to the Boston Braves and the young men who will train at the Myrtle Beach Wigwam, Home of Future Braves."

Many of us enjoyed spending a Saturday afternoon at the ball fields. Keith Cribb, retired Myrtle Beach school administrator, served as high school baseball coach in those years. Cribb, along with his players, recalls sitting near Bill Southworth, manager of the Boston Braves. Cribb said, "They gave us 12 dozen scuffed baseballs for our practice sessions."

The late Ernie Southern, a former catcher with the Detroit Tigers in the early 1930s, served as superintendent of the Myrtle Beach Schools. The Braves needed a centrally located ball field for special exhibition games. The high school field, which was located at the corner of 16th Avenue North and Oak Street, needed much improvement.

Southern said, "The Braves crew brought in clay and revamped the entire layout. They installed an excellent drainage system. It was one of the best fields in the state." In 1951, six Braves' Farm Clubs trained in Myrtle Beach. The teams were: Quebec, Eau Clair, Bluefield, Hartford, Hagerstown and Evansville.

DR. J. MARCUS SMITH

The training camp in Myrtle Beach closed in 1953, when the Boston Braves franchise was moved to Milwaukee. John W. Mullen stayed with the club. In 1966, the club relocated to Atlanta. In 1979, they named Mullen vice-president and general manager.

Mullen died April 3, 1991, at the age of 66. To honor his memory, the players wore the initials "JWM" on the left sleeve of their uniforms throughout the 1991 season.

John W. Mullen, a faithful and dedicated member of the organization, was the sole remaining link to the days when the former Boston Braves trained in Myrtle Beach.

VIII. The Growth Years   (1960s – 1990s)

Marcus and Frankie Smith (1960s)

The three of us grew up in the 1960s. Our neighborhood was a great one – full of many kids. We all loved sports, especially baseball. Many times we took our little red wagon down to the beach to get beach sand to line off our small baseball field in the backyard. We once put on a neighborhood ball game and charged admission. We even bought some snacks from the Ocean Pines motel across Highway 17 to sell at the game. Of course the parents and other children came to see us. Mom was the real sport. She loved baseball, and many times when David and I would not catch Frank when he wanted to practice his pitching (he threw too hard), Mom would put a sponge in an old catcher's mitt and squat down in the front yard to play catcher for Frank. She loved her boys, and she often said that she wanted nine boys so that she could field her own baseball team.

Mom and Dad were at nearly every one of our activities – be it school, sports or anything else. Dad was a member of all the various booster clubs. He was an assistant coach for the Yankees Dixie Youth League baseball team – and we were all on this team. Mom and Dad were very supportive of us in everything we did. We were truly blessed to have such devoted and dedicated parents.

DR. J. MARCUS SMITH

1967 Yankees team. Dad is 2nd row far right. I am beside him. Frank is 1st row, 4th from left.

Mom and Dad opened up their house to all of our friends. Of course, Dad loved the attention, and Mom loved having the kids around. Everyone was welcome, and our house served as a safe house for many kids who didn't have parents as wonderful as ours. Again, Dad was the practical joker, and Mom just enjoyed the activity.

We didn't take many vacations, but when we did we usually went to the N.C. Mountains. We went to Tweetsie Railroad in Blowing Rock, the Cherokee reservation in Maggie Valley and also Ghost Town in Maggie Valley.

We moved to a new house on Pine Lake Drive in 1967. But Mom and Dad kept the house on 38th Avenue and rented it out for many years.

1969 FUMC Church picture – plaids were in.

Marcus and Frankie Smith (1970s)

In the 1970's we began graduating from high school and college, and things changed a little. We were away from home, but our bedrooms were always there for us. We then began bringing our college friends by, along with our long-time friends. We would play basketball in the driveway, ping pong in the carport, table hockey in our den, and hearts card games in the dining room. You could even go fishing in the small lake in our backyard.

We planned and successfully pulled off a surprise 25th wedding anniversary for Mom and Dad in 1975. My future wife Sherry, who was a student at Furman with me, helped us plan the party while Frank and I were off at college. We had Mom and Dad's friends coordinate getting Mom and Dad away from the house long enough for us to decorate and prepare for the party.

In the late 70s, Sherry and I were married and lived in Columbia. Frank was in Optometry school at the University of Alabama-Birmingham. David was in Myrtle Beach and kept an eye on Mom and Dad.

Marc and Sherry's Wedding (1978) – David, Marc, Mom, Dad and Frank

DR. J. MARCUS SMITH

Marcus and Frankie Smith (1980s)

Sherry and I moved back to Myrtle Beach in 1980 (and rented the house on 38th Avenue for almost two years). Frank graduated from UAB and moved back to Myrtle Beach in 1982, and he bought into Dad's optometry practice. We were all back home once again, and Mom and Dad were quite glad of that. Mom continued to have hot dogs for lunch on every Saturday, as she had done for as long we can remember. We never knew who would join us, as everyone was always welcome to drop by. Mom would just throw a few more hot dogs in the pot. The simple pleasures really make for special memories.

Mom and Dad became grandparents of mine and Sherry's two boys in the late 80s. Marcus, our older son, was named for Dad's father. Will was named for Sherry's family. "Ging" and "Pop" became their grandparent names, and they were wonderful grandparents.

Mom, Dad, Frank, David, Sherry and Marc at a Smith family reunion (1983)

Marcus and Frankie Smith (1990s)

Frank and David both married and started their own families in the 90s. Frank and Maria married in 1989 and then had two daughters Anna and Luisa, and a son Andrew. David married Michelle in 1995, and they had a son Hilton. So, Ging and Pop had six grandchildren. Nothing pleased them more than having the whole family over for a visit or a meal. Christmas mornings were always special. In 1992, Mom and Dad moved back into the house on 38th Avenue North – after David had completely re-built the house on the same foundation.

DR. J. MARCUS SMITH

Seems Like Yesterday

On July 5, 1997, my wife and I attended a Statler Brothers' performance at the Palace Theater.

Before curtain time, we visited with folks from North Carolina. A party of 40 had chartered a bus and traveled to Myrtle Beach for dinner and the show. They planned to return home the same evening. They told us that the Statler Brothers would not be appearing in Raleigh. They remarked how fortunate we were to be living in such a fabulous resort city.

It wasn't always that way.

The census recorded Conway's population as 2,947 in 1930. As a first grader, I recall the summers without air-conditioning. We slept with our windows open, hoping to catch a cool breeze on a hot night. On weekends, beach traffic moved slowly in front of our house on Main Street.

In the quietness of the night, as enthusiastic tourists headed for Myrtle Beach, they crossed over loose planks on the Kingston Lake Bridge. The bump-bump-bump sound of the tires reverberated throughout the town. I remember thinking, someday I will live where those people are going.

In 1930, the population of Myrtle Beach was less than 500. Entertainment and recreations developed slowly along the coast. The Ocean Forest Country Club (now the Pine Lakes International Country Club) became home to the first golf course. The Ocean Forest Hotel had a grand opening in 1930. In 1935, the first edition of *The Myrtle Beach News*, a weekly publication, rolled off the press. The Myrtle Beach State Park opened the same year.

Earlier, Myrtle Beach Farms had erected a large two-story wooden pavilion on the oceanfront. The upstairs had a spacious hardwood dance floor, with a stage for performing orchestras. Bowling alleys were on the lower level. Mr. Robert McMillan operated a small, but colorful, carousel on 9th Avenue at the boardwalk.

In the mid-1930s, the Broadway and Gloria Theaters opened in Myrtle Beach. State blue laws allowed Sunday movies in the resort town. Washington Park Horse Race Track, with pari-mutuel betting, arrived on the scene in 1938, the year that Myrtle Beach was incorporated. The track closed in 1947.

People enjoyed dancing under the stars at the Ocean Forest's Marine Patio, which featured big name bands. In 1953, The Ocean Forest ballroom was home to The Circle Theater, which presented its plays in the round. Original Broadway players appeared at the theater.

Since 1990, the Grand Strand has entered a new boom with the emergence of a flourishing music/entertainment theater industry.

It wasn't always that way. We have arrived.

IX. Today and Tomorrow (2000s and the future)

Marcus and Frankie Smith (2000s)

In October of 2000, we had a 50th anniversary party for Mom and Dad. We invited family and friends and held the party at Pine lakes International Country Club, which was quite appropriate as "The Granddaddy" was about their age and it represented Myrtle Beach in its early years. We had a fun time preparing for the party and it was well worth it, as Mom and Dad thoroughly enjoyed visiting and celebrating with everyone.

Mom and Dad with their children and grandchildren

Unfortunately, the last few years were tough, as Mom and Dad declined in their health, particularly Mom. David and Michelle took charge when Mom became unable to use her legs. They moved into the apartment behind the house on 38th Avenue and lived there for 18 months, so that they could take care of Mom and Dad. They made it possible for Mom to stay in her house until the end. Mom was always extremely clear and bright in her thinking – and she was that way until she passed away on April 29, 2005. The entire family was there throughout her final evening. Everyone, including all the grandchildren, was able to see her and visit with her that evening.

Dad did remarkably well after Mom died. He lived for over three years – all with a broken heart. They had been close friends since elementary school, and ultimately married for 54 years. Dad really missed Mom – she was the strength of the family. He soldiered on as best he could. At the end, Dad moved in with David and Michelle at their house in the country. Again, they shouldered the responsibility and took care of Dad. He caught pneumonia and had complications in the hospital. We brought him home to the house on 38th Avenue North for the last one-and-a half days of his life. He died on May 16, 2008.

DR. J. MARCUS SMITH

Final Thoughts

Mom and Dad are no longer with us, but memories of them are still so strong. They were wonderful people. As for being parents, we could not have had better. As I have said before, they were always there for us. They treated each one of us as the unique individuals that we are. They gave us the foundation we needed for life. We just hope we can do them proud.

ABOUT THE AUTHOR

Dr. J. Marcus Smith was a native of Horry County. He grew up in Conway, graduating from Conway High School in 1942. He then went to the University of South Carolina for a year before heading off on a train to Southern College of Optometry in Memphis, Tennessee.

He married his childhood sweetheart Frances Marian Johnson in 1950, and they raised a family in Myrtle Beach (three of us boys). He practiced optometry for fifty years. He was very active in the community – with our activities, the Jaycees, Methodist Youth Fellowship (MYF) leader at the First United Methodist Church in Myrtle Beach and the Horry County Historical Society.

He wrote many articles on his two hometowns – Conway and Myrtle Beach – most being published in *The Sun News* newspaper. He loved this area and all of its rich history.

He loved people and thoroughly enjoyed talking and interacting with them. He and Mom (collectively known as "Ging and Pop") were wonderful grandparents – they were always available to baby-sit and help out as needed. They had six grandchildren who all lived near them. Family and friends were very important to them. They were married for over 54 years. Mom passed away three years before Dad. He was never the same again – they were indeed one together. They have been greatly missed.